# The Heroine of Cameron Dam

## The Annotated 1929 Memoir of Myra Dietz

### Sybil L. Brakken

# The Heroine of Cameron Dam
## The Annotated 1929 Memoir of Myra Dietz

**Badger Valley Publishing**
**45255 East Cable Lake Road**
**Cable, Wisconsin 54821**
**BadgerValley.com    715-798-3163**
**treasureofnamakagon@gmail.com**

Most of James and Sybil Brakken's books are available only at select outlets and at their website, **BadgerValley.com** where you'll find discounts and secure, online credit card ordering. Badger Valley Publishing offers *free shipping* to all USA and APO addresses and pays your Wisconsin sales tax.

**Badger Valley** can publish *your* book, too! Reasonable rates. Fast processing. Inquiries welcome. More at **BadgerValley.com** where you'll see images and excerpts from all of our 13 titles.

**As with all Badger Valley books, *The Heroine of Cameron Dam* is written for adults but suitable for young readers.**

Excerpts from this book and James Brakken's 12 titles can be found at **BadgerValley.com** where you'll find special discounts and free shipping to all USA and APO addresses.

*"Indie" Authors, James and Sybil Brakken, would like your help.*

Unlike writers who offer their books to "brick and mortar" publishers, independent authors rely on their readers to share news of their work. If you enjoy these stories, please recommend them to your friends, family, and your local community and school library.

Give your favorite Brakken book a five-star review on Amazon. Simply Google *James Brakken Books*, then choose the Amazon link.

Facebook users can "like" the Brakkens' 13 books at **www.facebook.com/jim.brakken** where you'll see the latest news about our "up north" novels and short story collections.

**Thanks for your help!**
*James & Sybil Brakken*

*In appreciation …*

Thanks are due to **Jim Ferguson,** president of the Sawyer County Historical Society, and their devoted volunteers who work tirelessly to keep our Northwest Wisconsin history alive. Your contribution is priceless!

Special thanks to **Karen Duffy** for the many hours she spent researching the lives of Myra Dietz and her siblings.

Thanks, too, to the **Wisconsin Historical Society,** the **Rice Lake Public Library,** and the **Winter Public Library.**

And thank you, **Priscilla Dietz Anderson,** for offering clues that helped round out our research into the lives of your Aunt Myra, and your grandfather, John F. Dietz, the defender of Cameron Dam.

Thank you, **Dan Mercer,** grandson of Leslie Dietz, for use of the stereopticon images from Myra's 1911 slideshows.

Thanks also to the many independent bookstores willing to offer self-published authors your shelf space. Your service to readers and writers does not go unnoticed.

Extra special thanks to my award-winning author-husband, James, for inspiring me to bring Myra's memoir to light!

*And thank you, readers. I sincerely hope you enjoy this annotated version of the memoir written by Myra Dietz nearly a century ago as much as I've enjoyed bringing it to you.*

*Sybil Brakken*

***The Heroine of Cameron Dam*** is the memoir of a young woman, Myra Dietz, caught in the middle of a violent land dispute between her steadfast father and the world's largest lumber syndicate.

Here you'll discover Myra's story in her own words and with very few edits made only for the sake of clarity. Some of the unusual spelling and punctuation she used reflects the writing and speech of her time. In order to offer a more authentic glimpse into Myra's life, I've left most of her examples of old-fashioned writing intact.

This book is more than recollections of a girl growing up on a Northern Wisconsin farm a century ago. It's an in-depth look at the persecution of the family of a working man who demanded his back pay from perhaps the most powerful industrial syndicate ever. But rather than settle, the lumber barons chose to use their influence over the county, state, and federal government to brush him aside. The result shocked a nation into realizing the overwhelming power of companies that then monopolized the USA was far beyond control.

Myra's memoir is an amazing glimpse into the past and the wrongs wielded upon American workers over 100 years ago. It's also a look into the world of this girl, Myra Dietz, and the life she lived on the family farm.

Sybil Brakken

~ ~ ~

*In memory of Maddie, our dear, sweet Golden Retriever.*

Madison Brakken
2005 - 2020

Sybil L. Brakken's
# The Heroine of Cameron Dam
## The Annotated 1929 Memoir of Myra Dietz

```
THE LIFE STORY
OF
MYRA DIETZ
OF
CAMERON DAM
```

Memories of John Dietz' feud with the lumber
interests at Cameron Dam, Wisconsin, as
recalled by his daughter, Myra Dietz

# PREFACE

Here at last is a reliable and truthful story of the John F. Dietz family, of Cameron Dam, in Northern Wisconsin.

Although the events narrated in this book took place many years ago, I have found that our melodramatic story is still fresh in the memories of thousands of people. Everywhere I go, I am asked to relate our experiences as they actually happened and always I find that the hearer has retained a memory of "an outlaw family of squatters" instead of realizing the truth. Our name and our fame will go down through the years in Wisconsin history, and I feel that a true account of our wrongs and sufferings, together with an explanation of our ideals and our principles for which we stood so firmly, should be preserved for posterity.

My father died three years ago, leaving no record in writing: my brothers, who stood so valiantly by my father in his fight, are now too busy to write the story of our lives, so I am left to tell the story of things as they actually happened at Cameron Dam.

Thousands of newspapers which carried stories of our feud hailed me as "THE HEROINE OF CAMERON DAM", because I, like my brothers was always near my father in every encounter. Perhaps it was for that reason that I was so cruelly shot down in ambush in 1910, when three of our father's enemies, with blackened faces, shot at my brothers and myself as we drove our team to town for the weekly mail, singing lustily from sheer youthful gayety as we trotted along in the October sunshine.

And because I was a "Dietz", the District Attorney of Sawyer County refused to serve a warrant on the sheriff and his posse who had shot us, I have suffered with and for my father. Therefore I feel that I am logically the one to give our family story to the world.

Laden with my family scrapbooks, which my mother carried from our home after the house and all its furnishings had been riddled with bullets, I went to the home of my friend, Peggy Kemp Lyon, where we turned my reminiscences and my stock of family data into a readable story. I have not exaggerated, I have not omitted anything: My method of putting the story together consisted in going over the story of our lives, month by month, year by year, and writing it down: I made no attempt to arrange a climax or follow any technique--so unique is our family's story that it formed its own high spots and left us with the "living happily ever after" ending:

It is not unusual to find melodrama in the North Woods, but it is unusual to find a man pitting his feeble strength against a great lumber company over the possession of a small dam over a bubbling little creek, and forcing that lumber company to spend a good portion of a million dollars to overcome him. Actual expenses of the company ran close to two hundred thousand dollars, and nobody knows-- unless it is the corporation heads-- how many more thousands were expended in bribes and "payments" to grafting county officials.

My father lost--in the sense that he was imprisoned in a travesty on justice for trumped-up charges-- but three years before his death he was pardoned by the Governor of Wisconsin, with the full restoration of his citizenship. This, in Wisconsin, means that my father was finally exonerated of all the charges, indicating the Governor knew them to be false. And in the years that followed, not one of the many "warrants" which led to the final battle at our log home, was ever served: What became of them, nobody knows.

The memory of my father's steadfast adherence to his rights will always be bright—we suffered much because of them, but we honor and revere him for his firm stand.

I will let the reader determine for himself whether my father was right or wrong. I hope the story will prove entertaining enough to keep him reading that far.

MYRA DIETZ

# CHAPTER I

My parents on both sides were children of pioneer settlers of Barron County, Wisconsin. On my father's side of the family they were of German and Pennsylvania descent.

My father's father, John F. Dietz, the First, was born in Hessendermstadt, Germany. He came to America at the age of nineteen years, his parents having died when he was a small boy, leaving him and a younger sister under the guardianship of an uncle.

They were heirs to a large fortune, which was to be divided between them when they became of age. His uncle had control of the fortune in the meantime, and made life most unhappy for the two young people. In fact, conditions became so unpleasant that my Grandfather Dietz decided to come to America to escape both his uncle and the military service to which he had become eligible. He promised his young sister that he would return for her when he had made his fortune in the new world, and one night, with only the clothes on his back, and a small amount of money, he ran away to a boat that was sailing to America. He was hidden by the boat's crew until it had left German waters, and from that point he worked his passage to America.

He remained in New York for some time and then later went to Saratoga Springs, New York, where he met and married Almira Schwartz, daughter of a wealthy Saratoga Springs businessman. This is the grandmother whose name I bear. After my grandfather Dietz became an American citizen, at the age of twenty-two, he returned to Germany to secure his fortune and to bring his sister back to America, fulfilling the promise he had made to her.

During the voyage to Germany, he met a man whose story coincided almost exactly with his own and who was returning to his native Germany for practically the same reasons. They traveled together for the remainder of the trip.

Upon reaching Germany they spent their first night at a tavern. When it became known among the guests that they were recently from America many persons gathered about them to hear them relate their experiences and to learn of the marvelous freedom in their newly adopted country.

Standing apart from the others, and listening with intense interest, was a German officer in disguise. He heard them tell of the Great America for a time, and then suddenly stepped forward, ordering them to cease spreading such propaganda, and placed them under arrest. Without any trial, or opportunity for legal defense, they were placed in prison, where my grandfather remained many months.

At last someone carried his story to the American consul, and his plight was immediately investigated as he was a naturalized American citizen. His release was secured through the efforts of the American consul, and he was advised to return to America immediately and avoid further trouble regarding his evasion of military service. He was given about half of his fortune—a sum amounting to $20,000, but he was obliged to leave without seeing his sister Elizabeth. He was able to get a note delivered to her, however, telling her to leave Germany on a certain boat and meet him in New York.

I well remember my grandfather telling how he sailed for America, carrying his entire fortune mostly in gold and silver. He had purchased a considerable amount of jewelry, which was about half the price in Germany that he would have to pay for the same articles in this country. Both the gold and jewelry were carried in bags which he quite nonchalantly left in his stateroom while he went to his meals and walked the deck during the six weeks it took to cross the ocean. Among the jewelry which he brought to this country was a solid gold watch and long chain which he brought to his bride, Almira, who had had no word of her husband during his long confinement in the German prison. This watch and chain are still treasured among our family heirlooms.

The story of my Grandfather Dietz' sister, my great Aunt Elizabeth, while it has no bearing on the story, is another of the family chronicles to bear out the tradition that "The Unusual" always happens to the Dietz family.

My grandfather went from Saratoga Springs to New York the day the boat carrying his sister was scheduled to arrive. When he reached the dock, the passengers had all left the boat, and although he ascertained that his sister had been aboard he was unable to find a trace of her beyond Castle Gardens, where the emigrants were sent at that time. He searched the streets of New York, and advertised for many weeks, but his sister was never located. He knew that his sister had been carrying her fortune with her as he had carried his own, and at last he gave up in despair, thinking she had probably been murdered for her money.

It seems strange, in these days, that a girl could be so completely lost when she earnestly desired to find her brother, but conditions were vastly different, one hundred years ago.

Some of my earliest recollections are the memories of my grandfather weeping over the loss of his sister. His heart was sincere and tender and he was inclined to "show his feelings" much more than my father or myself would have felt quite right. I recall my grandfather as a wrinkled, grizzled old man, with tears pouring over his ruddy cheeks as he told of his sister's loss.

Our family traces its rugged health back to this dear old man, for he was never sick a day in his life until three weeks before his death, which occurred in his eighty-ninth year. His hair was thick and bushy as a boy's, and beautiful with its snowy whiteness. His German chin whiskers were equally white. He never had a tooth extracted and his sound, white teeth were always a marvel to his friends and relatives.

At the age of eighty-one, he came to Cameron Dam to go deer hunting, with his son and grandsons. He carried a heavy, double barreled old shotgun that he had owned for a half century, but he shot a fine big buck weighing two hundred pounds.

"Py kolly, but dot deer did run!" he said when he came back to the house and related his experience.

It was my good fortune, in 1914, when I was lecturing on our experiences at Cameron Dam to learn the story of my Great Aunt Elizabeth. A young man came to the platform and told me that his grandmother was Elizabeth Dietz. By comparing notes, I found that she was indeed the long-lost Elizabeth. She had died in 1901, so my grandfather never saw her, but it was a great comfort to him in his last years to have the mystery of her disappearance cleared up.

According to her grandson, who had heard her story from childhood, the German Elizabeth was bitterly disappointed when her brother failed to meet the boat at New York. Not knowing a word of English, bewildered and confused at the sights and sounds of the new land, and heart-broken because of her brother's non-appearance, she presented a most forlorn appearance when she met a fine New York family. She was taken into their home as a daughter, and when they emigrated a few years later from New York to Menomonee Falls, Wisconsin, they brought Elizabeth with them. Shortly after that she married a son of the family, John Bloedel, and for two generations her family lived at Menomonee Falls, a scant hundred and twenty-five miles from the home of my grandfather and his descendants. And her life was filled with regrets that she never saw her brother again!

Returning to my Grandfather's family—after the birth of two sons, William and Henry, in Saratoga Springs, my Grandfather Dietz and his wife, Almira, emigrated to Winneconne, Winnebago County, Wisconsin. My grandfather had a small fortune, which seemed tremendous in those days, and they lived peacefully and happily in a little four room frame house in the little village, until the outbreak of the Civil War. My grandfather was drafted into service in the early days of the War. While he was away, their third son, John F. Dietz, the Second, was born on April 4, 1861.

This was my father! Small wonder that he had a war-like spirit, ready to defend his home and his principles against the invasion of the enemy, in his years of manhood!

At the close of the war, my grandfather returned to Winneconne, but the after-the-war-restlessness could not be calmed, and in 1870 he and his family emigrated to northern Wisconsin, taking up a homestead in Barron County. There they were one of the few white families in that portion of the country, their only neighbors being the rough inhabitants of logging camps and native Indians.

My grandmother, Almira, must have found life in the North Woods, vastly different from the cultured refined home she had left in her native New York. White women in those regions were indeed a rarity, most of the white men engaged in the lumbering business in that country being married to Indian squaws. In rude shacks, constructed by the lumber companies, or in native tepees, the neighbors of the Dietz family lived in the crudest of back woods lives. Food was cooked over open fires in the clearing before the cabins, or in open fire places. Moccasins and clothing for both men and women was made from deer skins by the silent brown-skinned squaws.

The Dietz boys worked with their father, clearing away the virgin forest from the land, carrying away the rocks, until the homestead was a well-tilled prosperous farm, producing good crops. While her husband and boys were thus employed, my grandmother was far from idle. After carding the wool which my grandfather sheared from the sheep, she spun it into yarn and then knitted the family sox or wove the blankets and clothing used in the home. Their log home was one of the largest in the community and it had one luxury that set it quite apart from the other homes in the community—it had an organ! Because of that churchly adjunct, coupled with my grandmother's deeply religious feeling, Sunday school and "church meetings" were held in the living room of the Dietz home. Most of the Indians had embraced the Catholic faith through the efforts of missionaries, but in my grandmother's classes were many little round-faced Indian children, some of them full-blood Indians and many the offspring of the inter-marriages. Even after the community had grown to great proportions, and church buildings had sprung up in the clearings, my grandmother Almira continued to play the organ and lead the choir at all church services. Our family treasures include hymn books and a little old brown leather bible which the staunch undaunted Almira used in conducting church services in her own log cabin home.

I have devoted considerable space to the story of these pioneer people for I believe it has a direct bearing on the lives of my father and our own family. The pioneer instinct in the blood of the Dietzes could not be denied, and years later when we went into the wilderness at Cameron Dam we were merely carrying on as our forebears had done. It would have been far easier to settle down in a good community, with schools and close neighbors, but that was not the spirit. Even with wealth and culture my grandparents preferred to battle for their existence in the rude North. Yet they must be given credit for refusing to live as other families—they took their refinement and education with them and sought to live decent, orderly lives, uplifting those about them rather than sinking with them.

Precisely the same spirit dominated our family when we went to the Cameron Dam wilderness to hew a home out of the woods. As the reader continues, he will see how we took our ideals and our principles with us. We wanted good government, good schools, and a good home. We wanted to live and let live, trespassing upon none and not being trespassed upon. But what a fight that meant!

# ONE FAMILY DEFIES EVEN THE U. S. IN DEFENSE OF CLAIM TO PROPERTY

(Special to The Press.)

MILWAUKEE, Aug. 13.—Backed by his rifle, his wife and his family of six children, John Dietz for two years has defied officers of the county, state and national governments at his cabin on the Thornapple river in the heart of the northern Wisconsin forest. Several men have been shot in battles waged in the woods with the Dietz family.

Thornapple river constitutes a dead line which Dietz boasts will be maintained until he is carried from the place feet first, his family dead and his rifle empty.

Dietz's position is based upon his claims to Cameron dam, over which the Chippewa Lumber & Boom Co., drives its logs. He demands a tollage of 10 cents a thousand feet for all logs schuted over the dam and for wages for $45 days in which he was in the employ of the company. In two years he has jammed 20,000,000 feet of logs in the Cameron dam

is inaccessible, although in the winter narrow sledges have been taken over the uncertain trail through the hardwood forest. The lonely family subsists on deer and other game shot along Thornapple river and the produce from the

# CHAPTER II

My mother was willing to accompany my father in his pioneering projects because her family, too, came of pioneer stock. Her father was Rufus L. Young, born in Richland, Oswego County, New York, June 11, 1839, of Yankee parentage. He learned the cooper's trade and when he was a very young man he came west and located at Neenah, Wisconsin, Winnebago County, where he worked at his trade. During the first year of the Civil war, my Grandfather Young married Mary Ann Brown, daughter of Chester and Mary Brown, also pioneer settlers of Winnebago County.

Perhaps my brothers, my sister and myself inherit our unfailing good nature and our ability to laugh at hardships from our great-grandfather, Chester Brown, our mother's grandfather. His obituary notice clipped from the Neenah newspaper when he died at the age of seventy-four said:

"He had the happy faculty of friendship for all and his jovial manner made him a favorite with all with whom he came in contact"

In the second year of the Civil War, my mother's father, Rufus Young, enlisted at Oshkosh, Wisconsin, with Company 1, Thirty-second Regiment, of Wisconsin Volunteer infantry, and served until the close of the war. He marched with Sherman to the sea. He was in the distinguished battle at Shiloh, and in the siege of Vicksburg. As an officer under Sherman, who in 1864, took command of the army in Georgia and forced General Hood to evacuate to Atlanta, he accompanied the famous Northern general on the march across the state capturing Savannah and Charleston, South Carolina. From this point they moved north, capturing the most important positions, and my grandfather remained an officer on General Sherman's staff until the close of the war.

I recall the stories my Grandfather Young used to tell of the hardships they endured during the war, how they marched for many weary miles without shoes living on hardtack, and sleeping at night with logs for pillows in pouring rainstorms. One of his favorite tales was the story of coming upon a deserted Confederate camp and finding a luscious baked potato, partly crushed by a careless heel print. My grandfather carefully picked up the potato, and after picking off the leaves and dirt which clung to it, he divided it with his brother, Azro, who was in the same company, and the two boys enjoyed their first potato feast in many months.

Those of us who have spent our lives in Wisconsin can appreciate the craving for potatoes which the Wisconsin soldier boys must have suffered. Potatoes form one of our chief articles of diet, being the chief product of our state as our soil is particularly adapted to its cultivation.

At one time, during the course of a battle in the woods, Azro was seriously wounded. My grandfather saw him fall, and at the risk of his own life, he ran to him, picked him up and carried the wounded lad several miles back of the battle front where he could be given medical attention. My grandfather, however, went through the war without a wound, but the hardships and exposures left traces which he carried until his death, at the age of eighty-three.

After the close of the war, my grandfather returned to his home at Neenah. On December 26, 1866, my mother, Harriet E. Young, was born, and during the following years five other children were born.

In 1872, my Grandfather Young, his wife, and the two children which had been born up to that time, emigrated to Barron County, Wisconsin, in a covered wagon. The distance was two hundred and seventy five miles and it took them two weeks. They carried bacon and other provisions with them, filling their water jugs from the crystal clear streams and lakes they encountered along the way, and shooting the occasional squirrel which peered inquisitively at the strange sight of a team and wagon in the great silent woods. Only a trail was marked through the trees, but the hardy little family made the journey without mishap.

Arriving in Barron County, my grandfather found employment with the Knapp-Stout Company, a logging concern, serving as a carpenter. His cooperage knowledge served him well, for his work was building the logging sleighs, axe handles, and other equipment used in logging operations. He worked for them for three years and then took up a homestead of one hundred sixty acres in the neighborhood of my Grandfather Dietz' family. The Dietz family had been settled in the community for two years, when the Young family arrived. Thus the two families which had come from the same state, New York, and had lived in comparatively close range of Winnebago County, met for the first time.

The two children, John F. Dietz and Harriet Young, destined to go through such a melodramatic episode as the Siege of Cameron Dam, went to school together from early childhood. Outside of school hours they played together, and together raced to the roadside to see the great clumsy stage-coach come lumbering by, or to climb over the sides of the big wagon that hauled provisions from the nearest railroad point, sixty-five miles away, to the little settlement. My mother always laughs and says she would have said anyone was crazy if they told her she would one day marry John Dietz. He was six years older than little Harriet Young and delighted in pulling her long black braids in school and otherwise making life miserable for the little girl.

When they went wading in Dietz Lake, he would hide the girls' shoes and stockings, or he would float out to the middle of the lake on an improvised raft and frighten the girls into hysterics, only to paddle himself to shore an hour later by his agile feet and legs.

It was a wholesome, hearty, healthy life those youngsters lived, giving them a physique and endurance able to withstand many hardships in later years.

Then on February 9, 1882, in the town of Stanley, Barron County, Wisconsin, Harriet Young and John Dietz were married. At that time Harriet was fifteen and the bride-groom was twenty-one. Harriet's hair was coal black and her long curls were done up in a "French twist" on the back of her head for the first time on her wedding day. John's hair was golden yellow. The bride's wedding dress was of gray silk, made with the basque in style at that time and two stiff ruffles which projected in bustle-fashion. Around her neck she wore a white silk kerchief, edged with fine silk lace, and held in place by a gold pin. On top of her head she wore a tiny lace cap, similar in appearance to a lace handkerchief, pinned in close folds. Her long tight sleeves were shirred from shoulder to cuff, and the front of the basque and skirt was trimmed with a four inch band of shirring which formed a continuous line from the neck to the hem. The hem, let me add, reached the floor.

The bridegroom's suit was the conventional black swallow-tail, and his wing collar and white tie completed a correct wedding costume. With such stiff heavy costumes, the two youthful faces in their wedding tin-type look strangely incongruous, like children dressed for a play.

But the wedding costumes had to be correct! Sixty-five guests witnessed the wedding and sat down to the bountiful wedding dinner. Both families were prominent in the community, and the wedding was celebrated in a manner appropriate to their wealth and reputation.

A year after their wedding, the young couple bought an eighty-acre farm adjoining the homestead of her parents. It was necessary that the young wife remain near her father for she continued to act as his secretary. He was clerk of the school board, chairman of the county board, and successively held many important positions in both town and county. He was a charter member and helped organize the first Masonic Lodge in Barron County.

Soon after moving to their own farm, their first child, Florence May, was born. The sixteen year old mother and the golden haired father stood proudly by while the baby, in a christening gown of lace and ruffles that reached to the floor, when held in the arms of her aunt Leanna, was christened "Florence May Dietz". Within six years three other children were born. These were Harry Eugene, Clarence Hubert, and myself, Mary Almira. I was born October 30, 1888 on a bright sunny Indian summer day, and was given the names of my two grandmothers, Mary for my Grandmother Young, and Almira for my Grandmother Dietz. However, I was called 'Myra" from my earliest childhood by everyone except my Grandmother Young, who always called me "My"—a nickname which would certainly win the prize for brevity.

Since this is a story of my life, it might be fitting to mention a few of my childish characteristics which have become family tradition. I was the "little one" of a family of big sturdy persons, quick as a cat, so my grandmother Young always declared. I know that my hair was black as night ever since I can remember and I utterly failed to inherit the

least trace of my mother's beautiful curls.
Straight and long as an Indian's were my black
braids, but they were well suited to my fat
red cheeks. Those cheeks were always my
despair, I did so want to be pale and
interesting-looking, but what could I do with
cheeks like apples. To make matters worse, my
mother usually dressed me in bright red
dresses, which made my cheeks look all the
redder. I was proud as could be—other children
would pull off their shoes and stockings at
school to "go barefoot", but not I! No one
ever saw me doing anything so undignified as
walking barefoot. My grandfather and
grandmother Young aided and abetted me in my
childish pride. I remember when I was about
seven or eight years old, I went to them and
explained seriously that I just simply
couldn't go to the school picnic or speak my
piece at the last day of school wearing the
heavy boys' shoes which had been bought for
me. Of course, they were the regulation shoes
for little girls in the country, for girls'
and boys' activities in the woods were closely
akin, but I felt they didn't harmonize with
the ribbon sash and hair ribbon that I was to
wear with my good dress to the picnic. My
grandparents listened to my story with all
seriousness and a few days later they came
with the team and wagon and took me to town,
Rice Lake, five miles away. In the town they
took me to the best shoe store and to my great
joy fitted my feet with golden brown slippers—
and slippers were rare in those days because
the summers were so short that folks
considered you didn't "get the good out of low
shoes". Then, to make my happiness complete
they bought me a pair of fine lisle stockings

to match. To this day I never hear the song, "Oh, Dem Golden Slippers", without thinking of those wonderful shoes. But truth compels me to add that the new shoes didn't help my oratory. In the midst of my "piece" I grew nervous and confused, and after fussing with my dress and sash and looking down at the new shoes for what seemed an interminable age, I gave up and ran wildly from the platform.

# CHAPTER III

By the time I was eight years old two more
children, Leslie John, and Leanna Rosella, had
been added to the family. Leslie was a year
and a half younger than myself and he upheld
the family honor in "speechmaking", where I so
grievously failed. By the time he was five
years old, and just as broad as he was long,
he could stand up on a platform and deliver
the longest and most serious of speeches. His
memory was perfect, and his enunciation was
slow and deliberate—no Friday night Literary
Class at the school house was complete unless
Leslie Dietz was present to give one of his
favorite "pieces". Leanna proved to a chubby
little round-faced, blue-eyed body, with
beautiful chestnut brown curls. She was more
quiet and reserved than the rest of us—
probably the shadow of the terrible tragedy
which took her from us when she was eight
years old was already thrown over her little
life.

Our life on the little eighty-acre farm
next to the homestead of our grand-parents was
the happy normal life of country children of
that period. My father was in the stock
business, importing untrained western horses
and selling them for a good profit after he
had broken them to harness. Our farm was a
good one, and about that period of my life, my
mother—who was always the family financier—
acquired two more farms, all under
cultivation. All together, we were in far
better circumstances than most of the pioneer
families. Our home was still a five room log
cottage—but all homes were of logs in that
country—and ours was well-built and

surprisingly comfortable. It was well heated with stoves through the long winters—for wood was plentiful.

Our recreations were few, of course, for we were country people and the automobile and paved roads had not appeared. In the summer there were picnics, attended by the whole neighborhood, and the high shining spots of the Fourth of July, the last day of school and Circus Day. The three older children were usually allowed to accompany our parents to the celebration and to the circus, where they feasted both eyes and "tummies". We youngsters had to stay at home to await the years when we would be old enough to go, but we were always well rewarded with candy and nuts when the family returned from these expeditions.

The Literary Classes at the schoolhouse, which I mentioned before, were the highlights of the winter season. These classes were usually composed of the older girls of the school, who trained the younger ones to sing songs and "speak pieces" and to act in simple dialogues. Oftentimes little plays, with the characters carefully costumed in weird outfits made by the youthful actors, were put on, and these were banner nights. The parents of the school children were urged to perform along with the youngsters, and as my father sang bass and my mother was a gifted soprano singer, we Dietz children were often thrilled by the well-applauded efforts of our parents. Leslie, as I have said, was also a star performer at these affairs. Whole families—and families were families in those days—would come to the school house in huge bob-sleds, with sleigh bells jingling merrily, and the country would resound with the cheery greetings and the gay laughter as some mittened, fur-capped farmer would sing out a particularly apt joke and receive a quick stinging reply from a witty tongue. The Friday night classes were the only opportunities, outside of church when a certain amount of decorum must be preserved, for the country folks to meet and visit, and many a recipe for head-cheese and the quickest way to turn the heel of a sock were exchanged in shrill feminine whispers while the singing was going on.

Perhaps our lives had some hardships—perhaps many discomforts—but somehow we didn't realize it. We thought life was very good, indeed.

The high spot of the year, however, was Christmas. The same method of celebration was observed year after year, but it never grew stale. We always saw a fine big pine tree brought into the house on the afternoon before Christmas—a tree so straight and green that it was worthy of the miles of popcorn and cranberry chains we had been stringing for weeks in anticipation of its coming. Huge popcorn balls, some made with white sugar, some with brown sugar, and some with molasses to give different tints, were also ready for the tree. Then we had tinsel and little tin candle holders which clamped on the tiny branches like an old fashioned clothes-pin, carefully saved from year to year, ready to make the tree the gayest of the gay!

The tree was never decorated in our presence. We youngsters were put into a bedroom, supposedly to go to bed, but who could sleep at such a time? Instead, we sat around the fire and told stories and laughed at our childish jokes, until ten o'clock. Then my mother would come slipping into the room to tell us that father was out at the barn seeing to the stock, but that everything was ready for Santa Claus and she would wait with us until he came. Utterly breathless we would sit in the bedroom until we heard a loud knocking at the door, and the loud clatter of sleigh-bells (oftentimes it was the clatter of a bunch of table spoons if the real sleigh-bells couldn't be taken from the harness) and a deep, gruff voice would roar a hearty "Good Evening!" Amid much stamping of feet and jangling of bells (or spoons) he would call for my mother, and when she had entered his presence, leaving a wildly excited little group in the bedroom, we would hear him ask how many children were in the family, and if they were all good boys and girls! How we hung on her reply, as each one recalled some little incident during the year when behavior might well have been improved! At last we would hear her re-assuring answer, and we would be called in a few minutes.

What a sight for our childish eyes! The huge tree, resplendent in tinsel, with glowing candles, and glistening festoons of red and white, interspersed with silvery balls suspended by cobwebs. What if they were only the chains of popcorn and cranberries we had ourselves strung—and the balls were the well-remembered popcorn balls dangling by white threads.

It was a slice of fairyland itself to us! And, marvel of marvels! There was Santa Claus himself, with the well-known red suit, the white whiskers and the huge high boots that his photographs always show.

After a word of greeting and a jolly "Good-bye", old Santa Claus would depart with a grand flourish of sleigh-bells and more stamping of snowy feet at the doorway. Then a few minutes later our father would come in from another door, with a word of anxiety concerning the welfare of the stock in the barn, and would register great disappointment when told of Santa's visit which he missed. Then, at last we would be calmed down sufficiently to turn our attention to the presents under the tree. Warm mittens and stockings knitted by our mother and Grandmother Young, caps and knitted stocking caps for the boys and warm wool dresses for the little girls. And usually among the presents, we little sisters found red eiderdown hoods, trimmed with bands of otter or beaver from animals trapped in our own woods. Candy and nuts in bountiful profusion were found under the tree—and it was a sticky-fingered, tired little cluster of youngsters that the Sand-man found in the wee small hours.

It seems a far cry from this happy, cheerful, home-loving farmer, entering so heartily into the spirit of that Day of Days, to the man described in the following clipping, taken from the *Milwaukee Free Press*, July 31, 1906.

"John Dietz, the Cameron Dam farmer who has successfully defied authorities of Sawyer County, will never be taken alive. He is a dead shot, and he shoots to kill. The man who would attempt to capture Dietz must expect to kill him first or get killed. That is the opinion of the Milwaukee members of Sheriff Gylland's posse, who returned yesterday after a week's unsuccessful siege of the defiant farmer. They say that it will require either the cooperation of several scores of sheriff's deputies, or a company of militiamen to capture Dietz!"

One reason for the appearance of this little book is to clear my father's reputation of the charge that "he shot to kill".

The first Fourth of July celebration I ever attended was at Rice Lake in 1897 when I was nearing my ninth birthday. It was the first time the entire family had enjoyed a Celebration, and my mother spent days before the Fourth starching and ironing the best clothes of her six youngsters. The great Day was almost upon us, but with only twenty-four hours to wait, I suffered an accident which almost prevented our going. Perhaps it was an omen intended to keep us at home, and protecting us from the tragedy which our innocent little excursion precipitated. On the third of July the bees swarmed! Anyone who has ever been near a bee-hive knows the loud buzzing and frantic darting flight of the cloudlike swarm of bees accompanying their queen on her journey to new quarters. This continues, of course, until a fresh hive is prepared for them. While my father was engaged in the delicate operation of putting the queen and a few of her followers into the new hive, so the others would follow, I ventured too close to the swarm, and one of the busy little insects landed on one of my rosy chubby cheeks and stung me severely. The morning of the eventful day found me swollen like the proverbial poisoned pup and unpleasantly sick and feverish. Grave consultations concerning the advisability of our going were held, but it was finally decided the other youngsters should not be disappointed and I begged to go, too, so we went.

It was a great day, with foot races and tugs of war and all the well-known amusements of a country celebration. The fireworks were awe-inspiring beyond words, and as we jogged along our five mile trip home about midnight, we felt that life could hold no further wonders—that we had indeed seen everything!

Five days after our great celebration, four of our little ones were stricken with a disease known at that time as Black Diphtheria—Harry, May, Clarence, and Leslie—my two older brothers, my older sister and my younger brother. For some reason, I was spared—maybe my bee-sting had made me immune. We had a good doctor, Doctor Valbey, who was a personal friend of my father, and who attended us most faithfully. Despite his good care, however, my brother, Harry, died on the tenth day after our Fourth of July Celebration. He was buried that same night in the new little gray suit my mother had bought for his Celebration trip. In those days in that locality, embalming and the various mortician activities were unknown, and the victims of contagious diseases were merely washed and dressed before being placed in a casket encased in a rough box and rushed to the grave in the dead of night. We had no funeral

service for my bright handsome brother, Harry—
only a prayer offered up by the health officer
who came with a one-horse wagon to take the
casket to the cemetery. Only my grandfather
was allowed to accompany the body, and the
grief-stricken parents turned at once to the
task of saving the other children, who lay at
the point of death.

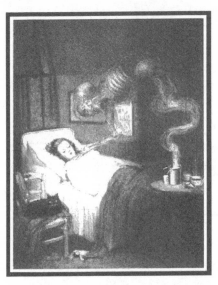

Known as the 'strangler of
children,' diphtheria spreads via
human contact, causing a thick, gray
to black film to build in the throat
and larynx that chokes the patient.

Children were most susceptible
to the disease. Parents regarded
diphtheria as a death sentence. By
the late 1880s, intubation devices
became available to doctors, saving
many victims' lives. Vaccines
developed prior to WWI helped
bring the disease under control by
the 1920s.

At last, they recovered and the house was
fumigated by the Health Officer, and the
quarantine lifted. My sister, May, was quite
well again—as were my brothers—and was playing
in the hayfield in which my father was working
about three weeks after my brother Harry's
death. Suddenly, she complained of illness and
my father carried her into the house. The
doctor was summoned, and to his great dismay,
he found that she was again afflicted with the
terrible diphtheria. Again we were
quarantined, and this time, after May's
recovery, the Health Officer declared our
house must be burned to the ground, with all
bedding, books and wearing apparel.

We moved our furniture into the new granary which my father had just completed, and one hot summer day the Health Officer came out and touched a match to the comfortable old log home in which all of us had first seen the light of day. We stood around and watch it burn, and then took up our residence in the granary while the new house was being built. The town allowed us one hundred dollars for the burning of our home!*

*The burning of a home to remove the threat of black diphtheria from a community was a common practice in the late 19<sup>th</sup> and early 20<sup>th</sup> centuries.

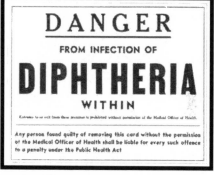

DANGER
FROM INFECTION OF
DIPHTHERIA
WITHIN

The new house was a frame building, one of the first frame homes in the locality. It had six rooms, with the bedrooms on the second floor, and boasted the first concrete basement in the whole countryside.

Two outstanding events connected with the building of the new home remain in my memory as vividly as though they had happened yesterday. One was a runaway in which my brother, Clarence, had a narrow escape. He was sitting in the wagon-seat holding the reins of the horses, while the workmen filled the wagon-box with rocks from the farm land. Although only ten years old, he considered himself quite a farmer, and driving a team was the first desire of a farm boy. Suddenly an angered bumble-bee, dislodged from his home among the rocks, alighted on one of the spirited horses and stung it. The runaway commenced, and pell-mell, through the woods and across streamlets, the frightened horses ran. The huge rocks, so carefully collected to build the foundation for the house, were bounced high in the air, and scattered far and wide over the pathway of the runaway. Clarence tried to hold them with his sturdy little arms, but at last was forced to abandon the effort, and he climbed backward over the bouncing load of rocks and fell from the rear end of the wagon to the ground. He had bruises and scratches galore, but no serious injury.

The other event was the making of my first enemy! After the foundation had been built and the masons were putting in the basement floor, I was walking around the edge of the house foundation, counting the rocks and collecting the beautiful golden shavings which curled so invitingly around my arms and fingers—looking for all the world like real jewelry to my childish imagination. I must have stepped on the corner of a particularly slippery rock—it might have happened that my foot gave it a little push, too—but anyhow, the rock tumbled right down into the basement and cut a big gash in the head of one of our neighbors, Victor Olson, a big two-hundred-pound Swede. It was the nearest I ever came to getting a good spanking—my father shook me and demanded to know how it had happened. But I was always a good talker, and I spun an alibi as fast as a present-day speeding motorist, telling him the rock rolled down just through the force of gravity and my toe had nothing to do with it. My father believed it, but not Victor! Ever after, he looked at me with cold blue eyes and muttered Swedish phrases that were anything but complimentary.

When the house foundation was completed, a building bee was held. The neighbors for miles around came with hammers, saws, and nail boxes, and constructed the entire frame of the house in one day. What a busy place that was! The pounding of nails, the hum of saws and planes, interspersed with the good natured chaffing of the workmen as they commented causally on the worthlessness and laziness of each other.

In these days of highly specialized employment, it is refreshing to think of those sturdy farmers, who were capable of being veterinarians, teamsters, stockmen and business men, and who were also able to build a house when the occasion demanded.

We moved into our new home the latter part of September, 1897, and on November 2, 1897, my sister, Helen, was born. She was the seventh child—perhaps that mystic number had something to do with the important part she was destined to play in our later life at Cameron Dam. But, at any rate, we knew nothing of that then, and she grew and thrived like any other farm child until she was two years old. Then she had a severe illness, and on New Year's Eve, the doctor operated upon her as she lay on the kitchen table and removed half a rib.

I mention these tragedies of our early days because, as we look back over them now, it seems that Fate kept us alive to suffer as severe buffeting as any family ever endured. Medical knowledge was not then as it is today, and human lives hung by a frail thread, indeed. But somehow, the members of our family survived more than ordinary illnesses and we were each able to play our part in the tragedy of Cameron Dam.

The Dietz Family
at their Thornapple River farm

Above, Leslie & Clarence
Below, Helen, John, Myra, Stanley, Hattie, & Johnny
1904

# CHAPTER IV

During the four years following the birth of my sister, Helen, our family life was a busy happy one. Father was clerk of the school board, town chairman, and during those years he was Senior Warden of the Masonic Lodge at Rice Lake. He loved animals and had made a study of them so he was the local veterinarian. He made no charge for his services—rather he did it to relieve the suffering of animals which might have gone untended.

One night he was returning from lodge when he saw a beautiful bay horse, belonging to our nearest neighbor, standing with his broad breast uncommonly close to the wire fence. He instantly felt that something was wrong, and upon investigation found the horse had been caught in the wire and was slowly bleeding to death from cuts on the breast.

My father raced his team to our home, hastily secured his veterinary needles, which he sterilized in carbolic acid, and taking my brother, Clarence, and myself to hold lanterns, ran back to the injured horse. I can remember the beautiful animal quivering in every muscle, but he stood quietly while my father sewed up the great cuts from which the blood was gushing. My brother and I held our lanterns firmly so the light would not waver, and we always felt that our firm steady lights did as much as our father's efforts to save the life of the horse. After the sewing operation, the horse was led gently to our own barn, where my father remained with him all night, and in a few days he was on the way to recovery. The owner was deeply appreciative—

but my father refused to take any payment for his veterinary services.

My father continued his stock business, on a trifle larger scale each successive year. Our farm was well-tilled, good roads had come in, and we had seen little villages spring up about us. In addition, the railroad was being extended beyond Rice Lake, our shopping center, five miles from our farm. My father sold ties to the railroad company, and all winter long a crew of men worked in the wooded portions of our farm, clearing the logs and cutting them into ties. We were prosperous and happy.

The two farms which my mother had acquired—as mentioned in a previous chapter—were heavily wooded, and these tracts were logged during these years.

Our recreations were simple, but heartily enjoyed. My father played the violin at all school affairs, and at all the country dances. Not only was he proficient at playing the fiddle", as it was known in those days, but he made his own violin. The first three or four lacked that "something" which made them successful "fiddles", but at last he made one that was a real sensation. It was purchased by a violinist of national reputation, and the last report we had on this instrument was that he valued it at several thousand dollars. How we would love to obtain possession of this violin and keep it among our family treasures! My father made many other violins for different people, he was never again able to approach the tone and quality of that earlier one. He kept the last one he made, which was an excellent instrument, but this was stolen when our house was looted after the Cameron Dam siege.

As soon as the roads were opened up in the spring of 1900, a book agent came to our farm home to see my father about putting a certain publisher's books in the school, of which my father was school clerk. He remained over night with us, and while there was so delighted with our comfortable home and good farm that he started negotiations to purchase it. My father was willing to sell it, because three of us had finished the country school, and he felt that it would be advisable to move on one of our other farms, closer to town, so we could attend the high school at Rice Lake. The book agent's wife came out to look at the farm, and she, too, was delighted with it, so they purchased it about March 1, 1900, for $1800 cash, possession to be given May 1, of the same year.

I would like to add at this time that the farm was sold fourteen years later for $17,000.00, and last year the man who owned it refused an offer of $60,000.00 for it. He has built a beautiful home on the land, but our old home is one wing of the building.

A month after the sale of the farm, while we were still living in the home, my sister, May, was married to Herman Voigt, a prosperous young farmer of the same community. Sixty-five guests, mostly relatives, attended the wedding ceremony. May's godmother, our Aunt Leanna, wife of W. W. Dietz, the oldest brother of my father, was in charge of the wedding festivities. Our uncle was sheriff of Barron County for many years, and our school vacations were always spent at their home in the jail building. It was a big old brick

37

building, and we had many glorious times
romping about its queer corridors and narrow
little iron stairways with our cousin, William
Dietz, who was later to attain fame as a
nationally known football coach, "Lone Star"
Dietz.*

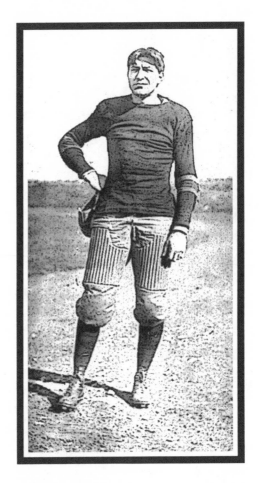

*Myra's cousin, William "Lone Star" Dietz, coached football at Washington
State, Purdue, Louisiana Tech, U of Wyoming, and other colleges, plus the
NFL's Boston Redskins, a team named in his honor because he claimed to
be part Sioux. Dietz's claim remains controversial. A Washington court
found him guilty of masquerading as a Native American in order to avoid
the draft during WWI. Lone Star Dietz was inducted into the College
Football Hall of Fame as a coach in 2012

As the wife of the sheriff, our Aunt Leanne was "out in the world" and consequently knew better how to conduct such important society events as weddings than my mother or sister. So Aunt Leanna brought over the woman who always assisted at her own parties, and the wedding feast was cooked and served in great style.

Our Aunt Leanna had a natural talent for doing things correctly, whether it was serving dinner to a chautauqua lecturer, conducting a women's club meeting, or cutting over an old silk dress for one of us girls. My mother always gave Aunt Leanna great credit for keeping us neatly and nicely clothed. Aunt Leanna had better clothes than a great majority of the women in the county, for she was naturally a fastidious dresser, and about twice a year she would bring over all the dresses which she wished to discard. Then what a week of sewing we would have! All the dresses would be cut down to our size, and the three of us would step out to church and country parties in haughty grandeur.

Although my sister, May, was Aunt Leanna's god child, and my sister, Leanna, her namesake, I was the favorite of her family, and for years they begged my parents to let them adopt me and rear me as the sister of their little boy, William. But the number of children in the family did not make one of them less precious, and their offers were always rejected.

My sister, May, was sixteen at the time of her marriage, and her boy, Jesse, was born a year later on the farm which the youthful bridegroom's father had given them as a wedding gift. This made members of five generations of our family living at that time, and we received much newspaper comment, as it was—and still is—quite uncommon to find five generations living.

After the wedding was out of the way, we commenced packing to leave the old farm and move to the new place. It required a month's time to transport the stock and house-hold goods to the farm which was known in the community as "The Old George Place." We loved the new place, not only because it was closer to town, but because the home was beautifully situated in a great grove of tall stately pines.

My father bought one hundred head of sheep that spring and put them out to pasture, as he wanted to give up farming and go into the stock business on a more extensive scale than ever before.

Another baby, Stanley, was born a month before we left the old place, and my mother had plenty to do in settling her brood into the new home among the pines. There were six of us then, for Harry had died just three years before, and May had married and gone to her own home, leaving, Clarence, myself, Leslie, Leanna, Helen, who had attained the age of three years, and the new baby, Stanley, named for the town where my father and mother were married.

By the thirteenth of July, 1900, we were comfortably settled and already anticipating the opening of school, when another tragedy befell us. My sister, Leanna, then eight years old, came in from play one day with a tiny scratch on her knee. She complained of a severe pain there, and a sick headache. My mother thought it must be her childish imagination for so tiny a scratch couldn't hurt much! But she thought it best to humor the child—as she would say—and accordingly bathed the scratched little knee with hot water. Instantly it swelled twice its size, and the scratch became more plainly visible. My brother, Clarence, went for the doctor when the child went into convulsions. The doctor came out to examine the child, and hastily returned for his surgical instruments. He returned to our house late in the evening, and for the second time within a year a member of our family lay on the table in the lamp-lit kitchen to undergo a severe operation. Leanna never recovered and at eleven o'clock she died. Her body turned spotted, and then the doctor knew that the tiny scratch, which seemed so harmless, had been the bite of a poisonous snake.

She was a beautiful child, with round chubby face, hazel-gray eyes, and long chestnut curls which tumbled around her shoulders. Again my Aunt Leanna was called in, and with her own hands she made the fine little white lacy dress in which my little sister was buried. We had always attended the Methodist church, but Leanna's funeral was held in the Presbyterian church with the Reverend W. P. Burrows officiating. Reverend Wm. Palm, pastor of the Presbyterian church, had lost his own little daughter just a short time before, and he said our tragic little Leanna reminded him so much of his little girl that he simply couldn't preach her funeral sermon. The church was packed, and everybody tried to shake our hands and express their sympathy at our loss.

Our friends were many in the community, for we were a thrifty, prosperous family. We were jovial and good natured, ready to laugh, sing, play the violin, or "speak pieces" when the occasion demanded. My father and brother, Clarence, were always ready to help in "building bees", threshing, taking care of the crops where the farmer was ill at a critical time in his farming operations, and, as we have mentioned, in caring for sick or injured stock.

My mother, despite her numerous children, was active in church work, and never-failing in her attendance of quilting bees, and other feminine gatherings. She helped cook and serve at all Masonic and Eastern Star festivities, which stamps her as a shining light in the culinary world, for only the best cooks in the community were called upon at these important occasions. Her greatest reputation was as the maker of "oyster stews" for the winter parties—an oyster stew simply wasn't anything unless "Hattie" Dietz made it!

# CHAPTER V

After the death of my sister, Leanna, we acquired a fear of our beautiful farm home. We didn't know how or where Leanna had been bitten by the snake, and we were afraid to step out lest one of the rest of us should become a victim. We hated the whole farm.

My father had become discouraged—so much illness and the deaths of Harry and Leanna made him think a sort of jinx was following him. He thought that we might be better off if we would leave the farm. Accordingly, we moved into the village of Rice Lake, where we children attended school, and my father made trips to and from the farm each day to feed and water the stock.

My father made a hunting expedition each year into Sawyer County, in northern Wisconsin, where he hunted and trapped on a tract of land forty miles from a railroad. He was always talking of that land, praising its beauty, its fertility, its great trees and its advantages when the future was considered. He felt that it would be a wonderful place to live—a marvelous heritage to his children. To his great joy, he found on one hunting trip that the tract of land was for sale. It had belonged to Hugh L. Cameron, who had recently died, and had come into the hands of his widow. The case had been brought to probate court, and she wished to dispose of it because there were several minor heirs. The tract of land consisted of one hundred sixty acres on one side of the Thornapple River and forty acres on the other side of the river, between which was the famous Cameron Dam. Accordingly in 1900, my mother purchased the tract of one hundred sixty acres, and the Chippewa Lumber and Boom Company acquired the forty acres, about the same time. My mother paid $500 for the tract of land she obtained.

Thus in the autumn after we had moved into the little village of Rice Lake, my father went hunting on the land which had become their own. While hunting he met John Mulligan, foreman of all the lumber camps and log driving activities of the Chippewa Lumber and Boom Company in Sawyer County, and visited him at the camp where he was then stationed. He told Mr. Mulligan that he loved that section of the country and would like to live there if he could induce his wife to come with him and bring the children. Mr. Mulligan said the company had recently put up two camps on the Brunette River, about seven miles from the tract owned by my mother, and also that there was a beautiful clearing, the North East one quarter of Sec. 9, Township 9-38 5, which he could buy from the lumber company for $2.50 per acre. Mr. Mulligan further said that a good reliable man was needed at Price Dam, which bordered on the clearing, and he believed if my father would go to Chippewa Falls during the winter to see a Mr. Chichester, manager of the Chippewa Lumber and Boom Company, he could get the job. He said the job would pay $2.00 a day the year around, and thus my father would be able to pay for the land with his wages. During the winter, after some correspondence with Mr. Chichester, my father went to Chippewa Falls and completed the arrangements for the land on that basis.

My mother bitterly opposed the move to Sawyer County. She felt that our education would be sadly neglected in the backwoods—the lack of social contacts and church affiliations loomed black and bitter as she looked into the future. We were all bright children, and it seemed a shame to take us into the woods where we could be scarcely less wild than the creatures in the forest. At last she gave her consent to the move, and in April, 1901, we moved to Sawyer County.

My father and the two older boys, Clarence and Leslie, took the work team, hitched to a sleigh (spring comes slowly to northern Wisconsin), and driving the flock of eighty sheep before them, made the trip to Price Dam, a distance of sixty miles. Almost the whole distance they followed along the beautiful Chippewa River, stopping at the regulation stopping places to feed and water the sheep and horses, and to stay overnight. In addition, there were many good farms along the way, where the farmer and his stock and his sons were made welcome. I remember one place in particular, for we stopped at the same place when the rest of us made the trip, where my father was allowed to drive his sheep into a big yard fenced with a tight rail fence. It was a sort of country tavern, known as the Brainerd Stopping Place, maintained by a farmer, his wife and daughter, and was famous throughout that part of the country for the warm hospitality and good meals given the traveler.

When my father had settled the stock and the sheep at Price Dam, he returned by train to get my mother and the children. We had a three-seated driving carriage, with a canopy top, bordered with deep fringe, and a fast stepping driving team. My mother, father, and we three children, Helen, Stanley and I, with our trunks and household paraphernalia deemed too valuable to make the trip with the stock on the sled, filled the carriage to a pretty tight fit, but the trip was made without accident. The first night out we stopped at the Brainerd Stopping Place, the second at Raynor's Stopping Place* and the following afternoon we reached our destination, Price Dam. We went immediately to the big lumber camp which was to be our home for three years. It was almost new, and was clean and comfortable. Although the lumber company had ceased operations in that neighborhood, they had maintained the building which became our home because it was needed in the spring when a great drive of logs was to be made. Then perhaps two hundred men would come to this dam, sleeping and eating in that building, while they put the logs through Price Dam.

The building was of rough logs, with the bark on the exterior but the inside was hewed and white-washed. It had a thick hewed floor close to the ground, with a cellar under one end for vegetables. My father immediately brought lumber from Larson's Bridge, the nearest stopping place, seven miles distant, and he and the boys built a stair-case and laid a floor for the second floor, making a good two-story building. Then they made partitions, giving us a living room, kitchen and bedroom downstairs, and three bedrooms upstairs.

*The term "Stopping Place" often referred to a lumber camp building that had been converted for use by travelers. Raynor's Stopping Place is on the Chippewa River at the intersection of US Highways 27 and 40 in Sawyer County and is on the National Register of Historic Places. Additional information on Raynor's Stopping Place can be found in the appendix.

Our home was a queer mixture of refinement and crudity. In the kitchen we had a huge copper sink, with a trough carrying the sewage down the hill to the river. In the living room we had a big dining table, over which was suspended a kerosene lamp in a chandelier arrangement glittering with glass prisms. When the family was alone, the table was large enough for our meals, but when company came, it could be extended with eight leaves, and seat twenty-five people comfortably. We had a fine organ, which had made the trip north in the sled, and my father built shelves to hold our books and the big clock. We had a big velvet rug on the floor, two smaller rugs of the same quality, and many small rag rugs which my mother had made. Our bedroom was comfortably furnished with beds and bureaus, and rocking chairs were comfortably scattered throughout the home.

Our home at Price Dam was located three miles from where the village of Winter, Wisconsin, now stands. Our nearest railroad point at that time was Hayward, Wisconsin, a village of about four-hundred people forty miles away. There my father purchased all our provisions and about twice a year he made the trip, taking the big carriage. In the summer time, the top had to be removed from that carriage, for the branches and dense foliage hung too low to permit its passage along the narrow road through the forest. Hayward was the county seat of Sawyer County, with only six other tiny villages scattered through the county at that time. Near Hayward was the big Chippewa Indian Reservation.*

*Lac Courte Oreilles Band of Lake Superior Chippewa Indians

We were once more happy and contented—it seemed that all our troubles had been left behind. The scenery was beautiful beyond my powers of description and the fishing and hunting were unequaled. We would row along the Brunette River as it meandered through the hills and the thick woods, and watch the deer who came down to the water's edge to drink and feed on tender roots. If we kept to our course, the deer would stand fearlessly and watch us as we rowed past them, but if we made a movement toward them they would "show the white flag" and dart quickly into the timber.

The river was very deep, and almost a mile wide in places, with a distance of five miles that we could traverse with a boat. It was a deep dark blue in color, almost black, which gave it its name. The dams were constructed so the fish could go freely from one stream to another, and nowhere else in Sawyer County could such bass and muskellunge be found.

My brothers and I would go out in the boat early in the morning, and they would row while I did the fishing. When I would feel the fish strike, one of the boys would take the line, and then the fight would be on! One morning we caught two fish, one weighing twenty-eight pounds and the other thirty pounds.

We had a good ice house on the shady side of the home, for it was an easy matter to cut blocks of ice three feet thick in the spring and pack it away in sawdust from the piles left by the lumber camps. Thus the big fish were never wasted, for we could keep them on ice until every last morsel was devoured. How delicious they were—brought from the cool depths of deep fresh water!

# CHAPTER VI

So beautiful was the location, with such fishing and hunting advantages that my father conceived the idea of establishing a summer resort there. He advertised in the sportsman's magazine, *Field and Stream*, and reservations began coming in immediately.

Most of the hunters and fishermen would bring their own tents, which they would pitch near the riverbank, and while my father and my brothers acted as guides for them, my mother and I would cook the meals. The fare we served was enough to make one's mouth water to think of it. Great slices of muskellunge, and crisp little bass, fried in butter was the chief dish three times a day, with occasionally a tender venison sirloin steak. Huge platters of fried chicken, thick custard pies and velvety ice creams would disappear like magic when the hungry sportsmen would return. We had our own milk cows, with plenty of cream and butter, and a garden plot with green onions, lettuce, radishes and all the small garden truck in bountiful profusion. For these meals we would charge from thirty-five to fifty cents.

Sportsmen from Chicago, Milwaukee and St. Paul came that first summer we were at Price Dam, and many hunters came from the same cities to get the two deer allowed by law during the autumn. My father always had great consideration for the deer and a deep respect for the game laws. Not long after we arrived at Price Dam, he found that lawless Indians and low types of white men were slaughtering the deer, merely to obtain the hides, leaving the carcasses for the wolves and vultures. They killed them at all seasons, oftentimes leaving helpless little fawns to starve to death, and thus rapidly diminishing the number of deer in the forest. My father saw that conservation was necessary to keep the animals from being exterminated and yet he, as well as other law-abiding settlers, needed fresh meat during the summer for the families, with the railroad so far away. Therefore, he wrote the State Game Warden, telling him of the practices in deer hunting, and adding that he disapproved of such lawlessness, but that it seemed necessary to kill an occasional deer out of season to furnish meat for settlers, and asking that the Warden make some ruling which would govern him and the other settlers. My father received a nice letter from the Game Warden, explaining that there was an unwritten law of the backwoods, which permitted settlers to kill deer occasionally for food, but the wholesale slaughter of the animals was most strongly forbidden. Soon after that the Warden arrived to investigate conditions in Sawyer County, and he found that some of the lumber companies would hire men to go out in the fall and kill dozens of deer which would be hung where they would freeze, thus furnishing meat all winter long to the camps and the lumber companies would be saved the expense of buying meat from the farmers.

This was my father's first step in incurring the wrath of the community. After that, several game wardens would suddenly appear in the county each year, and it was felt that my father was responsible for their coming. The sale of buckskin was profitable, and the chief source of income was cut off for many families, through the watchfulness of the game wardens.

The dam was under my father's care and received constant watching. The most important time in its care was the spring of the year, when the gates would be closed for several days before being opened to supply a head of water on the Chippewa River where the main logging activities were taking place. Two other dams were on the Brunette River, above Price Dam, and although they had watchmen, my father gave the orders when the gates were to be opened and closed. My father or one of the boys would row the boat five miles up the river, and then take a foot path around the flowage for a mile or so to the other dam to give notice. Then the message would be carried to the next dam.

However, it was necessary for my father to keep a watchful eye on the dam at all times. An Indian, or one of the white settlers, would open or close the dam to facilitate the passage of a boat over the rapids, or to make fishing better. Then, if someone were not in charge and right on the job, the gates might be left in the wrong position and thousands of dollars' worth of damage might be done in a short time through the force of the water. My father took his responsibilities very seriously, and if he were absent at any time, a member of the family kept an eagle eye on the dam.

This life continued for three years—the sportsmen came regularly in the summers and autumns and we thoroughly enjoyed our life in the woods beside the beautiful river. During this time we had no school, but my father bought books for us, and both he and my mother supervised our home study.

One outstanding event occurred during the time we spent at Price Dam. My father and mother returned to Rice Lake for a visit with our grandparents, and remained a month. I was fourteen at the time, and deemed quite old enough to be left in charge of my little sister, Helen, and baby brother, Stanley, one six years old and the other three. In addition to doing the housework, and cooking for my brothers, Clarence and Leslie, I cooked meals for travelers who stopped at our place, for by that time we had a good reputation as a "stopping place". My parents made an agreement with me whereby I was to receive all the money I took in for meals, and I made about thirty dollars in the month they were away. Considering that I only charged thirty-five cents per meal, it can be seen how many custard pies I had to bake, and the countless fish and chickens I had to fry.

When they returned, my mother carried a suspicious white blanketed bundle. I had seen four other little brothers and sisters, in tiny blankets, and I knew I was up against another big sister problem, and I certainly didn't relish the idea! I went out behind the woodpile and sat until dark, just as mad and unhappy as I could be. I didn't go near the baby for a month, much to my mother's grief. I was willing to do my household duties, but I refused to even look at that unwanted baby brother. But at last I was obliged to give in—the baby was the only blonde in our family of children, the only one to inherit our father's blue eyes and golden hair—and by the time he was a few weeks old his big blue eyes, his winsome baby smile, and his curly golden hair, together with his absolute "goodness", made me his adoring slave. He was named John, Junior, and was really John Dietz, the Third. To this day he is my favorite in the family, and his own little son, John Dietz, the Fourth, just a trifle over a year old, has as great a hold on my heart as his father.

Children were a real problem in the backwoods country. The little ones who could toddle around had to be watched carefully lest they stray into the woods and be picked up by a bear or hungry wolf. My brothers always carried guns to protect themselves, and even I was forbidden to venture far unless accompanied by my brothers or my father. At night all the stock had to be put into barns or in tight pens to protect them. Bears would attack the cows and calves, and wolves and wildcats were the particular enemies of the sheep. We never lost a sheep during the time we were there, which was an unusual record, but we found one fine heifer one morning partly eaten by a bear. The leader of our sheep was a fine old ewe, named "Nanny", and we could call or whistle for her and she would come trotting as fast as her little feet would carry her, the bell around her neck jingling a regular little tune. The rest of the sheep would follow her closely, and when they reached the pen the flock would be given the usual sheep food, but Nanny was given an extra portion of corn, or a lump of sugar. We always gave Nanny credit for saving the sheep in her flock but it might have been only her eagerness to get the "tidbit" that caused her to find her way home before dark.

Our family ties grew very close indeed, for we had only a few friends outside our own family circle. Our church and Sunday School was at Larson's Bridge, and we were more than friendly with the Larson, the Bishop, and the Egberg families. There were four or five children in each family, and we always went to their little school affairs, and picnics. Our parents were very strict with us, and didn't allow us to attend public dances or associate with many of the families in the community. In those days it was a real undertaking to get very far from home, and we didn't have an opportunity to make the acquaintance of many fine families in Sawyer County that we met in later years. By the time I had reached the age of fifteen, I felt that our parents were too stern for any use, and I began to long for a little more life and society than our backwoods life offered.

At the end of three years, my father thought he had sufficient money coming to him, as wages for watching the dam, to pay for the tract of land as per his agreement. But after some correspondence with the lumber company, he was told that the land had increased in value and they refused to keep their part of the bargain. My father then decided that we would leave Price Dam, and move to our own farm in Sawyer County, seven miles back in the woods. After several futile trips to Chippewa Falls to get either his money or a title to the land we had been living upon, he sent in a claim for 841 (eight hundred and forty-one) days of work, for which he was entitled to $2.00 per day through his agreement with the lumber company. But without waiting to collect his money, we moved to the log house at Cameron Dam which was to be our home through the stormy years when our name was in every newspaper.

# CHAPTER VII

My father had taken a prominent part in the Sawyer County election in 1902. The better element in the county thought it high time to oust the politicians who had been in power for many years. At the spring election, April 1902, the old group of officers, who had been fattening their own purses from the county funds, was overwhelmingly defeated.*

But another problem presented itself at the close of Election Day, when the defeated candidates refused to turn over the keys of the Town Hall. The Sheriff wired the governor that a militia was needed to quell a riot, and troops at Rice Lake were in readiness to make the trip. But a prominent banker wired the governor, cancelling the order, and my father took charge of the situation.

Standing on a table, he talked for several hours to the members of both "armies", and so convincing were his arguments that he persuaded the leaders of both sides to make peace and the keys were turned over to the newly elected officers. However, there were some followers of the defeated candidates who were not in favor of a peaceful settlement, and a plot against my father's life was carefully planned.

* Myra refers to the so-called "Courthouse Gang," controlled by county board chairman, Harry B. Shue. Shue catered to the wishes of the lumber barons who owned Hayward's immense sawmill, several stores, and the bank. They employed most of the men in Hayward, a true "company" town. Shue's daughter had married the county judge who, in turn, appointed her as clerk of court. An associate of Shue's kept the corrupt officials in office by bribing tribal members from the Lac Courte Oreilles reservation on Election Day, trading cash and liquor for their votes. Another Shue confederate, William Giblin, wore the sheriff's star and did Shue's bidding

Some of his friends learned of it and when my father returned to his hotel at Hayward, the friends suddenly appeared and after informing him of the plot quietly spirited him out to the edge of town where he found his own team awaiting him, and the road was guarded while he raced home. Hayward was the county seat, as I have mentioned, where the election was held, and our own home was forty miles away.

By the time we moved to Cameron Dam, in 1904, the candidates defeated in that riotous election in 1902 had again attained control of the county offices. That explains the prejudice of the county officials against my father at the beginning of the controversy at Cameron Dam.

In explanation of the conditions in Sawyer County both at the time we lived at Price Dam and Cameron Dam, we might quote the following clipping from the *Eau Claire Telegram*, written by August Enders, under the date July 26, 1906.

"To arrive at an intelligent conclusion one must not fail to look into the conditions of things in Sawyer County. The writer has been over the major portion of it and finds that from appearances it is one of the richest in the state. The whole thing was formerly embraced in one town called Hayward, but a recent legislative enactment has divided it up. The population in 1900 was 3,593, most of whom lived in the city of Hayward. Today there are about 1200 voters in the county. That there has been graft in the county is admitted by almost everyone, but it is perhaps not as widely extended as John Dietz has charged it to be. The graft consisted of fake land deals, robbing government land of timber, and buying the Indian vote which, if statements are to be believed, has swung more than one election. This, of course, would be easily possible in a county which contained so few voters. Officials have also often been charged with having been bought by the lumber companies. This may possibly be true in certain cases; one thing is certain however, that in times past there has been gross mismanagement in the offices of certain county officials whose names will not be mentioned in this connection. The way it is said the Indian vote in Hayward used to be bought was to give them all the drink they wanted and march them up to the polls in squads and after they had voted, pay them off. At the polls things were watched close enough to see they voted "right."

Mr. Enders is referring in this article to the election difficulties which my father sought to overcome.

Although our farm at Cameron Dam was in the backwoods, we had one hundred acres of it under cultivation. During the three years we spent at Price Dam, my father and the boys cut hay and harvested grain from it regularly. They had built a log house, stock barn, and a big root cellar. The house when we moved into it had three large rooms, and additions were made to it from time to time.

The Chippewa Lumber and Boom Company had been allowing their horses to graze over our Cameron Dam farm during the time we lived at Price Dam. My father did not object, at that time, but after they refused to pay his claim for wages, he felt that they were not entitled to any favors from him. Accordingly, he sent notice that the horses should be removed. Then, to make sure that he had the boundary line between the land belonging to the lumber company and his own farm firmly established so he would not trespass on their holdings, he made a crude survey of his farm with compass and lines, assisted by my two brothers. To his great surprise, he found that half the dam was on his land. About half the flowage (the portion of land inundated when heads of water are formed to take the logs through the dam) on our side of the river, and one half of the elevation built so teams could be driven across the dam proper were ours if my father's survey could be believed.

My father sat down that very evening at the dining table in the dining room and wrote a letter to the lumber company, stating that he was much surprised at the situation revealed by the survey, and asking that an authorized surveyor be sent to lay out the correct boundary line between their land and his own. He told them he did not wish to trespass on their land, and would be glad if they did not trespass on his.

In response to his request, the lumber company sent their head surveyor, Thomas Sergeant, with a crew of men to survey the forty acres owned by the lumber company. They worked all day running the lines, and the work was difficult for it was early in April, the

winter was just breaking up, and the men had
to wear hip boots in the slushy snow. My
father and the surveyor, of course, were
friendly and my father accompanied the crew,
watching them more from the standpoint of
entertainment than any idea of "spying".

When the work of surveying was finished,
Mr. Sergeant turned to my father and said:
"Well, Dietz, the Dam is yours!"

The survey had revealed the astounding fact
that the whole dam, together with the
elevation (which constitutes the wing of the
dam) on the southeast side of the river, was
on our land.

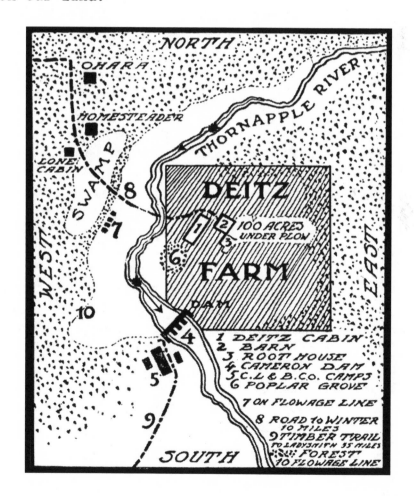

Mr. Sergeant and his men came back to our house—they had eaten dinner with us and left their traveling clothes at our home—and dressed to make the trip back to their headquarters. Mr. Sergeant's sox had become soaked inside his rubber boots. My mother gave him a pair from those she always kept on hand for father and the boys. When he was ready to return to town he told my father that he had been advised to ask the terms of settlement, if he found the dam to be on the Dietz property, as my father's letter had stated.

My father said that he wished to be fair, and all he asked was his wages for 841 days, which the company owed him for his work at Price Dam, and damages for the piece of land (about fifteen or twenty acres) which was under water when the heads of water were raised. In addition, he said he was entitled to tollage on the logs put through the dam from that time on, as the dam was ours.*

Mr. Sergeant agreed that my father's claims were fair, and said he was certain there would be no difficulty in coming to an agreement with the lumber company on those terms. However, he said, it would be a week before he could return with the money from the lumber company, and since a week's delay would be fatal to the lumber operations at that time, he asked that my father at once close the gates of the dam and obtain a head of water while he was at headquarters. The gates of the two dams above had been closed by the other watchmen and already heads of water were being formed to carry down the three million feet of timber which lay out above the first dam,

*The State Charter of 1874 declared that the owner of any dam used to sluice timber had legal right to claim ten cents per thousand board feet.

ready to be floated down to the Chippewa River as soon as the melting snow and spring rains made the heads of water strong enough. That was the reason for the haste with which the surveyor had been sent in response to my father's letter. It was a critical moment for logging and driving, as the dams needed every drop of the melting snow and rainfall to swell the heads of water. My father, eager to do what was right and glad that the controversy over wages was to be ended, sent the boys immediately to shut the gates of Cameron Dam and raise the head of water. The boys returned to the house before Mr. Sergeant left and he thanked them for their work, and then departed, promising to return in seven days.

For seven days, the gates were kept closed and my father watched the dam according to Mr. Sergeant's orders. At the end of that time Mr. Sergeant returned as he had promised—but with an entirely different attitude toward my father's situation.

"I am here, Friend John," he said, "with orders from headquarters to offer you $500 to give up all rights to the farm and the dam and move out, giving the lumber company full possession."

My father declared the offer ridiculous.

"Why should I give up the farm and the dam when I have improved the land, built buildings, hauled away stones and made it into a cultivated farm sufficient to support my family and feed my stock, for less than I paid for it at the beginning?" my father asked Mr. Sergeant.

"You are foolish, John," said Mr. Sergeant. "You know you are bucking up against a great corporation and if they get you into court you will lose everything you own. They can drag the suit along for years, and you know that would take money to fight them. It would be better to take a small sum and avoid any trouble."

My father came back at him with this answer—I remember it clearly because I stood near my father when he said it: "I am not looking for trouble. I expect to stay on my farm, till my soil, and support my family. All I ask is to be left alone and I assure you I will harm no one. If there is any trouble they will come here looking for it."

Mr. Sergeant departed without further words.

Late the same afternoon, Charles Peterson, sheriff of Sawyer County, arrived. By that time the head of water was so great that we could not cross on the footbridge and the only way anyone could come to our house or any of us get out to town was to cross the water with a boat, a distance of perhaps a half mile. When the sheriff and his guide from the village came to the water's edge they whistled loudly and our dogs, a water spaniel and a shepherd, barked loudly so our attention was attracted to the pair. The boys got into the boat and rowed across the water and brought the sheriff to the house.

When the sheriff entered the home, he carried a small mail bag over his shoulder, and as he placed it upon a table, he said: "Here's your mail, Dietz!"

We hadn't had our mail since we had closed the gates of the dam seven days before and the little package of mail was quite sizable, with letters, newspapers and magazines. Of course I

pounced upon it, and with my father began
sorting it out, when the sheriff spoke again.

"And in that mail, Dietz, you will find an
injunction restraining you from opening or
closing the dam, or in any way interfering
with the lumber company's head of water now
being raised. And then he added, "But it isn't
worth a damn—it is only a bluff!"

The injunction lay there on the table in a
blue envelope and was not taken out and read
to my father by the sheriff as required by
law.

Sheriff Peterson was one of the county
officials placed in office at the time my
father quieted the riotous election, and he
cherished a kindly and grateful feeling toward
my father ever after.

They continued their conversation for an
hour, discussing the conditions in Sawyer
County as they then existed, and other matters
pertaining to the lumber company's activities.
During that time the rest of us read our
letters and the newspapers.

Then the sheriff complained that his feet
were wet, and he, like Mr. Sergeant, was
provided with a dry pair of woolen sox. He
gave Clarence a tip of fifty cents when the
sox were brought to him—a little matter which
Mr. Sergeant had overlooked when he was
likewise provided. Then the boys rowed the
boat back across the water, taking Sheriff
Peterson to the point where the team and man
from the village awaited him.

Immediately after the boys returned to the
house my mother told them to go and open the
gates of the dam, releasing the head of water.

I want to make it clear right here why she
had the right to do this. The farm belonged to

my mother. The injunction had not been served on her—disregarding the question of its legality—and therefore she was at liberty to open or close the dam at will for it was on her farm. The lumber company had made no investigation to determine whether my father or mother was the rightful owner of the farm, and naturally supposed my father was the owner when they served the injunction on him. The boys opened the gates, and the water went out.

Nothing happened then outside our usual farm activities until a week later. Then, on the 3rd of May, 1904, Deputy Sheriff Fred Clark came to our home from Hayward. By that time Thornapple River had resumed its natural proportions and the Deputy Sheriff was able to walk across on the foot bridge. When he reached the house he said: "John, I have come on a friendly visit. I have no warrant but I would like you to go out to Hayward with me and let us get this matter straightened out. If you don't, I know they are going to get out a bench warrant for you, which calls for the body 'dead or alive' and if you resist them they will shoot you."

"If shooting is their game," replied my father, "I'm a pretty good shot myself!"

My father hesitated a moment, and he afterwards explained the thoughts which entered his mind while he pondered the situation. He knew the lumber company had the tremendous amount of timber out farther up the river, and that the two dams above Cameron Dam had the great heads of water waiting to drive the logs down to the Chippewa River. Although the head of water at Cameron Dam had been released, there was sufficient power in the other two heads to carry the logs past the

64

Dietz property—at least far enough to make it unnecessary to pay my father any tollage. Then they could build a railroad or haul the logs the rest of the way to the Chippewa River. My father figured that he would be detained in Hayward about a week—sufficient time for them to complete their operations.

"I will do no such thing!" he said to Deputy Sheriff Clark. "I have done nothing for which I should run down to Hayward. It is the third of May and my corn and grain must go in. I can't leave my business and run around the county at the lumber company's request. I have not violated any injunction, for the injunction brought to our house a week ago was brought to me, but the farm belongs to my wife and she is the one who ordered the gates opened and the head of water released."

He went on to explain that he had sent to Chicago for five-foot woven wire fencing and that had recently arrived. The boys had the fence posts out and laid in position, ready to fence in the field of corn, oats and the vegetable patches to protect them from the sheep and the deer who would wander in from the woods and eat off the tender cabbages, tomatoes and small grain. It was time to plant these crops and the fences must be in place before the tender green sprouts were above the ground. It was the critical week in farming operations.

Deputy Clark was a country man himself and he appreciated my father's position and his firm stand on his rights and departed with a friendly word.

Our family went on with our work and our daily farm routine.

Sheriff Charles Peterson

Sheriff Fred L. Clark

Sheriff William Giblin

# Chapter VIII

On the 10th of May, 1904, just a week after the visit of Deputy Sheriff Clark to our home, the following story appeared in the *Milwaukee Free Press*, headed as a "special from Chippewa Falls".

"SHERIFF IS MURDERED"
Slain by Desperado who Resists
Order Issued by the Court.
Escapes to the Woods.
Posse starts in Pursuit and
Desperate Fight is Looked For.

"William Elliott was fatally shot yesterday by John Dietz, who, with his family, has been holding up the Chippewa Lumber Company's drive at the Dam on Thornapple River, for the past two weeks with rifles.

"An injunction was issued against Dietz, but he paid no attention to it. He told the sheriff he did not care if President Roosevelt issued the injunction.

"Judge Parrish ordered Dietz arrested Wednesday. The sheriff was driven away by Dietz, and the Judge then ordered the sheriff with a posse to capture the desperado. Deputies Giblin and Elliott left for Dietz' home, believing they could effect the arrest without a posse. When the Dam was reached, Dietz rushed from ambush, ordered them to hold up their hands, and fired, fatally wounding Elliott.

"Dietz then hurried into the woods and has not been located, though the posse is scouring the woods. It is believed that Dietz will not be taken alive. The sheriff ordered his deputies to get the drop on Dietz and kill him if necessary. Dietz is a desperate character. For ten years he has lived in abandoned lumber camps, hunting, fishing and trapping.

"Dietz was sheriff of Barron County at one time.

"The dam in dispute was built in 1877 by the Daniel Shaw Company and was sold to the Lumber Company in 1882. The state legislature granted three special charters during that period licensing its operation. The Chippewa Company owns land on the north side, and claims that it has owned it for four years, although the company has a deed easement.

"Two weeks ago the Chippewa Company sent Thomas Sergeant to interview Dietz and found him desperate. He demanded ten cents per log for logs that had passed through the dam in the past four years. He wanted from $15,000 to $20,000* and refuses less and continued guarding the Dam with Winchesters.

"The logs are held at another Dam above Dietz', and cannot be brought to this city. Dietz frequently fired at men who attempted to get logs over the disputed dam.

"Elliott resided at Eau Claire. He was a son of Chief of Police Chubb Elliott, and was thirty-eight years old. He was once under-sheriff of Eau Claire County."

*The reporter exaggerates here. Dietz claimed less than $10,000.

Now I shall tell the true version of this incident, as I remember it as clearly as if it happened yesterday, and the reader may judge for himself how much truth was in the story as wired to the *Free Press* from Chippewa Falls.

In the first place, I would like to state that in the line referring to my father as "sheriff of Barron County" he is confused with his brother, W. W. Dietz, who had been sheriff for many years.

Elliott was not killed—he was merely lying under cover in the lumber camp for a few days—and could not have been shot by my father because my father never even saw these men. They didn't come any nearer to our house than a point four miles away, to our knowledge, and certainly my father had no time to lie in ambush awaiting the uncertain arrival of a posse to arrest him. We expected the men to come with the bench warrant, for Sheriff Clark had advised him of that, but the farm work was most important and my father went about his daily duties without any undue anxiety. We knew nothing of these men even starting out to our house until we read the foregoing story in the newspapers.

We were able to piece together the actual happenings through the story of our neighbor, Valentine Weisenbach, a homesteader who made a little clearing about his cabin in the woods three miles from us over a barely discernible little trail. Valentine came to our home frequently, for he had a brotherly feeling for my father since he, himself, was a German and my father's father had come from Germany. Then when we were busy with our farm work, the faithful Valentine would bring us our mail and provisions, and oftentimes assist us on the farm as he had only the small clearing and supported himself by working for the lumber company during the winter.

On that fatal 10th of May, mentioned in the newspaper story, Valentine was returning to his cabin from the home of another homesteader, making his way along the logging road. Suddenly he heard the creak of a big lumber wagon and the shouting of men's voices behind him. He had heard that a bench warrant was to be issued for my father, and instantly suspected these men were on that errand. With the natural caution of a woodsman he stepped behind a big pine tree to watch them as they passed him. He saw perhaps a dozen men in the big lumber wagon, joking and laughing about "taking Dietz" as they passed a bottle of whiskey from mouth to mouth. Valentine stuck his head from behind the tree to obtain a better view, and perhaps identify the men, and one of the members of the group saw him and shot at the tree, narrowly missing Valentine's head. Four shots struck the tree and the ground in front of him, according to Valentine's story. He immediately stepped from behind the tree, and waving his arms, and shouted: "I'm not Dietz; I'm Weisenbach"

He was allowed to come forward, and was questioned about the whereabouts of my father. He said he had no knowledge of my father's affairs, and couldn't say where he was that day. He then proceeded on his way, and the lumber wagon, with its load of men, resumed its journey to the lumber camp.

When they made their report a few days later, after spending the time at the lumber camp, they told that Weisenbach and Dietz had

fired on them from ambush, and the story in
the papers given at the beginning of this
chapter was the result of that report.

Elliott remained behind at the lumber camp
for a few days and then appeared to refute the
story of his death. He explained the false
story by saying the posse believed him dead
for at the first shot fired by Dietz he had
jumped from the wagon box and run into the
woods, where he became lost and wandered about
for several days, finally stumbling upon a
lumber camp which returned him to
civilization. He was hailed as a hero!

As an aftermath of this episode, Weisenbach
was arrested two years later on a charge of
being "Dietz' accomplice", and tried for
"attempted murder".

The following story concerning his trial
and sentence was clipped from a Chippewa Falls
newspaper, May 8, 1906:

"His neighbors in the Thornapple
District testified in Weisenbach's
favor, while the men whose lives he is
accused of having attempted to take are
willing to swear that he did shoot at
them. One witness testified that he
found four bullet holes in the wagon
box, and that Weisenbach, who wore
spiked shoes, kicked him. William
Giblin, former sheriff of Sawyer County,
was sworn into that office to bring
Dietz 'dead or alive' into court. It was
while going to the Dietz home that the
alleged shooting occurred.

"After being out for some time, the
jury found Weisenbach guilty.

"Shortly after being found guilty by
a jury of his "peers", Judge Vinje

sentenced Weisenbach to Waupun for twelve years. With neither friends, relatives nor money to help him fight the case, he remained in prison for six years. When he was finally pardoned, he left the community and was never heard from again."

Getting back to the time when the bench warrant was supposed to be served, I want to make it clear that we were not bothered. Evidently assuming that they had done enough in publishing the totally erroneous story of "Elliott's death", the matter of the bench warrant was dropped by the officials. We went about our farm duties as usual.

However, Sheriff Peterson, who had brought us the injunction in the mail, did not fare so well. He firmly refused to take any part in serving a bench warrant on my father, and when pressure became too strong for him, he resigned his office as sheriff of the county. Whereupon he was hauled into court, given a stiff fine, and sentenced to six months in jail by Judge Parrish. His "crime" was 'contempt of court in failing to serve process of the court in the case of the Chippewa Lumber and Boom Co. against John F. Dietz.'

Thus many other innocent persons, as well as ourselves, suffered through our controversy with the lumber company.

About the fifteenth of May, that same year, about two weeks or less after the Elliott story, my father was sowing oats in the field in sight of the dam, when two shots were fired at him. My father was operating a small seeding machine, turning a small crank to scatter the seeds from a canvas bag which he wore around his neck. He later laughingly declared they must have suspected he was carrying a machine gun. The shots came from the direction of the company's lumber camp which lay across the dam on the southeast side of the river. The camp was a quarter of a mile from our house, but as our house and barn stood on a high elevation, anyone at the camp could see all the activities about our house. My father paid no attention to the bullets and finished sowing his field as though nothing had happened.

Then a few days later we awoke one morning to find muddy angry waters swirling about our home. Fortunately the house and barn stood on an elevation and although the flood reached the foundation on the side nearest to the river, our doorway and the path to the barn lay on the other side and the water did not touch that point, although coming perilously close. My father and the boys rushed to the dam, and there found the gates had been closed and the locks had been taken away so the gates could not be raised. They knew then it was useless to try to save the dam, for the water was already running knee deep over the top.

The two dams above Cameron Dam had been opened and the millions of feet of timber in great logs were roaring, rolling and tumbling down the black flood. I have had many experiences in my life—even going through a terrific cyclone—but I never saw anything to equal the terrifying sight of those great logs as they whirled down from above and were kept in check by the dam as long as it held. For an hour we watched them come down and pile up higher and higher behind the dam. The water mounted higher and higher—every minute we expected it to reach the house and barn and hurl them from their foundations. It was a terrible sight, awe inspiring, indeed, to see those big logs handled as straws by the force of the flood.

Suddenly there was an explosion on the other side of the river where the lumber camp lay, and the dam broke. We knew that dynamite had been placed there to hasten the breaking of the dam, and also to take out the fill or wing to widen the stream if the dam, proper, did not prove wide enough to permit the passage of the tremendous drive of logs. Many of the logs were carried through the opening and scattered along the river bank at various points below. A portion of the logs, however, did a peculiar thing that we always said seemed planned by Fate.

When the dynamite exploded, only half of the dam gave way—the other half remaining staunchly in place. This gave the tremendous head of water, carrying the great drive of logs, a narrow channel only half the width of the normal river in which to rush on below. As a result an eddy was formed on our side of the river, and as the logs rushed through the narrow opening in the dam they swirled into the eddy, piling end over end, roaring and tumbling, and landing on our property. When the water went on, three hundred thousand feet of timber belonging to the Chippewa Lumber and Boom Company, one tenth of their spring drive, lay on our farm, high and dry.

According to Wisconsin law, when an event of this kind occurs and logs are piled on a farmer's land, the farmer is entitled to water damages and for damages done to his land by the presence of the logs. The Lumber Company must come to his farm and make settlement and pay for the removal of the logs. If this is not done, at the end of three years the farmer may advertise the logs for sale, and after selling them to the highest bidder at a public sale, keep the money.

The lumber company never approached my father to ask his terms of settlement, and the logs lay piled on our land three years. We children scampered over them—it was great fun to play on the giant staircases the logs formed—and we took pictures of them with our little camera, but not a single log was removed for any purpose. During that time when the logs lay on our farm, the lumber company built a logging railroad and while the snow lay deep and cold the logs which lay scattered for miles above and below our property were skidded out. These operations extended for several years, the last being taken out of the community during the winter of 1908-1909. The money loss to the lumber company was considerable, running into hundreds of thousands of dollars, which the company sacrificed rather than make a settlement with my father and resume their regular lumber activities. The dam could have been re-built for a portion of that sum, and the tollage paid my father would have been a mere fraction of that amount.

It was interesting to note, when the logs had finally been transported from the Cameron Dam District, the finality with which the Chippewa Lumber and Boom Company stated they were through forever with the Dietz situation. The Dietz situation, they stated with great emphasis, was now up to the county officials.

But those stories were to come four years later.

That autumn of 1904, seven months after we had moved to Cameron Dam, we were given a school. That was done despite the fact that our family was named as "outlaws" in the newspapers. My father and the boys built a log wing on one side of the house, and it was equipped with nice shiny desks and a big blackboard. Books were provided by the county, according to Wisconsin law, and the teacher's salary was paid by the county. The teacher boarded with us, and promptly every morning at nine o'clock the school was opened. We five children, Clarence, Leslie, Helen, Stanley and myself took our seats and worked at our lessons all day, with the regulation recesses and noon hour. We received no favors because the school was under our own roof.

Our teacher was J. C. Gates, of Rice Lake, and after teaching us three successive terms and living with us three winters, he gave the following to the *Duluth News Tribune* in Minnesota:

"John Dietz of Cameron Dam fame, who for the past four years prevented lumber interests from floating logs through his premises, in Sawyer County, has been badly maligned, and reports regarding his position and actions have been greatly exaggerated, according to J. C. Gates, a teacher who for three years has taught school at the Dietz home.

"Mr. Gates who will teach school in Northern Minnesota this year, is in Duluth today. Last winter his entire class consisted of the six Dietz children, no outsiders attended the school. During the time he taught there, Mr. Gates lived with the Dietz family, and he has nothing but good to say of them. He is convinced that Dietz is in the right and says that he will win out in the end.

"Dietz is not the ferocious man that the newspapers had indicated. He is quiet and peaceable, except where his rights are trampled upon, and even then he does not use his gun until all other means have failed. He is the father of six exceptionally bright children, and everyone of them, as well as their mother, will stand by Dietz. They love him dearly, and knowing him to be in the right, they will back him to the end.

"The oldest daughter, Myra, according to newspaper reports, is one of the best rifle shots in the state. As a matter of fact, she never fired a gun in her life, and is mortally afraid of one, covering her ears whenever she hears one go off. Her father is kindhearted and generous. No one is turned from his door hungry, and I have known of many occasions where his enemies were invited inside to dine.

"For a long time there was a camp of from twenty to thirty deputies maintained on the ground to capture Dietz. Most of the butter, eggs and milk they used were purchased from the Dietz family. The deputies for the most part were in sympathy with him, and had no desire to arrest him. They were making good money by remaining on the ground, and that is all they cared about. One cannot talk with Dietz five minutes without being convinced that he is in the right."

Mr. Gates' statement concerning the camp was quite true. The men stayed at the abandoned lumber camp across the river, from which our house was plainly visible. Thomas Griest had been appointed sheriff in Peterson's place and the men were deputized by him. We were not actually molested, but suffered many more than annoying incidents.

Many of our sheep and cattle died before we discovered that poison had been placed in the little salt licks scattered about the pastures. Then one day, when I was getting a bucket of water at the spring from which we secured our drinking water during the summer months, I took a drink of water and became violently ill. We found that our spring had been poisoned and were unable to use the water for a long time.

The only charges that could possibly have been made against my father were the trumped-up ones growing out of the alleged "shooting" of Elliott at the time the posse of men shot at Weisenbach behind the tree. If the men had any warrants against my father for "shooting an officer, resisting arrest and contempt of court", as was claimed, we were always at a loss to know why they were not served. My father made many trips to Hayward for provisions, both he and my mother went to Rice Lake for visits with relatives and often came in contact with officers of law with whom they talked on the friendliest of terms.

On February 11, 1905, the following story was published in a Chippewa Falls paper:

## 'BANDIT' DIETZ OUT VISITING

"John Dietz, of the Thornapple River Dam controversy, was in our city yesterday.-- *Rice Lake Leader.*

"Mr. and Mrs. John F. Dietz, of the noted Thornapple River Dam case, are visiting in this city for a week or two, the guests of Mrs. Dietz' parents, Street Commissioner and Mrs. R. L. Young.

"The above are interesting items to the people of Chippewa Falls. Very few items could more eloquently express the travesty of justice which appears to be existing in Sawyer County.

"The man who single handed stopped the drive of the Chippewa Lumber and Boom Company on the Thornapple River, who scorned the injunction of Judge Parrish, who finally is alleged to have wounded men who were sent to arrest him and has threatened to do violence to anyone who attempted to serve the criminal warrants now out against him—is quietly visiting at Rice Lake—posing, as it were, before the people of that good town as a much abused hero.

"Not far away at Hayward, the county seat of Sawyer County, sits the newly elected sheriff. Though he holds criminal warrants against this man Dietz, the sheriff is comfortable. He stirs not in the direction of Dietz. The two men who held the office of sheriff before him made no attempts to storm the Cameron Dam heights to effect a capture.

Why should he? He will keep the Dietz warrants and the Parrish ukase pigeon-holed a little longer—and wait developments.

"Former Sheriff Peterson, of Sawyer County, is taking his three daily meals in the county jail. He was sent there by Judge Parrish for his refusal to arrest Dietz, but he cares not. When he has served his sentence he thinks that the people of Sawyer County will rise up and call him blessed. Meanwhile he argues that he will sleep the sleep of the righteous.

"And Former Sheriff Griest, who was appointed to take Peterson's place, his boasts that he would capture Dietz or die in the attempt, no doubt serves to amuse the Thornapple Dam man, both at home and when he is making his customary visits in Barron and Sawyer Counties.

"It is not now a question whether John Dietz is right or wrong in his contention. It is a question whether the officials of Sawyer County dare to do their duty. The arrest warrants which are out against Dietz should be served. Dietz should be brought before the bar of justice. It is certainly time that Sawyer County's travesty on justice come to a final close."

Another incident occurred during the early spring of 1905, less than a year after the dam went out, which was widely commented upon in the newspapers.

Although we knew that a posse of men were ensconced in the lumber camp across the river we were not molested by them. We would see smoke coming from the chimney of what was supposedly a deserted building, and we could see men at the edge of our land peering at our house through spy-glasses.

Then, one day in April, two men came to our house in the clothing of cruisers. Cruisers, it must be understood, are men who are not actually surveyors but are investigators looking over land and uncut timber with the idea of buying or selling. One of the men represented himself as Mr. Jonas, of Jonas Bros. Mercantile Company, at Madison, a brother Mason, and he introduced his companion as an assistant who was helping him look over a tract of land in the vicinity with the idea of purchasing it.

Mr. Jonas was walking with a cane and hobbling along as he approached the house. He said he had sprained his ankle and wanted some liniment. My mother gave him some, and then he asked for fresh eggs and milk, saying that he was staying at the camp while they were in the neighborhood and he couldn't eat the fat bacon and salt pork they had there. My mother gave him the last fresh eggs in the house, with a quantity of cream and butter. Mr. Jonas then remained at the house and chatted in friendly fashion on a variety of topics with my father, never once referring to the Dietz case, while his companion went on to Winter. Then, taking his leisure, he went back to the lumber camp.

The next day they called at the house again, and were given more food. Then as they sat around the big stove talking with my father. Mr. Jonas suddenly jumped to his feet, saying: "Here is a paper I want to give you, Dietz!"

My father instantly saw that they were trying to make service of some kind upon him, and his strong right fist shot out, knocking Mr. Jonas into the corner. Then he literally booted him out of the door into the yard and Jonas got up and ran away.

"You have come into my home as a cruiser and a brother Mason. You are still a cruiser to me and not an officer. Take your papers and get out of my house," said my father to Mr. Jonas as he put him out. And when Mr. Jonas started on the run back to camp he was still grasping the unserved papers.

His companion, in the meantime, had made a move as though to hand some papers to my mother, but when he saw what Mr. Jonas was getting he abandoned any such idea and took to his heels, too.

The newspapers made much of the incident, for Mr. Jonas turned out to be a United States Marshall, and it was a clear case of "resisting an officer" in the columns of many papers. Others, however, published an article written by my father in which he set forth the facts of the case, and sympathized with him.

William Irvine, Chippewa Lumber and Boom Company Manager and Frederick Weyerhaeuser, President of the CL&B and the Mississippi Lumber Company. He ranks as the eighth-wealthiest American of all time.

# Chapter IX

In the meantime, the Chippewa Lumber and Boom Company had changed the name of its concern to the Mississippi River Logging Company, and Mr. William Irvine was manager. He lived at Chippewa Falls and the noted park at that city is now named for him.

During the summer of 1905, a few months after my father had forcibly ejected the so-called cruisers, Mr. Irvine came to Cameron Dam to talk to my father. Mr. Irvine was a prominent Mason and when he found out that my father was also a member of that fraternity he suggested that they allow David H. Wright, Grand Master of Masons in Wisconsin, to arbitrate the matter.

Why this was not done can be stated most clearly by reading the following letter of my father, published in a Milwaukee paper:

"The proposition to leave the dispute to the Grand Master of the Masons was made by Mr. Irvine himself. I told him if the Grand Lodge would beat my family and myself out of property rights it was the only thing that I would lie down for.

"Mr. Irvine appealed to the Grand Master, David H. Wright. Mr. Wright wrote me that if we would submit all the differences in dispute to him in writing, he would appoint five Past Grand Masters as a Board of Arbitrators and fix a time and place for the hearing.

"My answer to Mr. Wright was that as I understood the law, all the differences in dispute could not be settled by arbitration.

"The first question that would come up before the Board would be the title of property. Next they had accused me of 'murderous assault' on innocent men, neither of which, in my judgement, could be settled by arbitration. Next, that my wife owned the property and was not a Mason and I could not see where the Grand Lodge had any jurisdiction. Mr. Wright's answer was that the case had been misrepresented to him, and that he declined to take any further action in the case."

My mother's title to the land had been questioned—and the report that we were "squatters" permitted to live on the lumber company's land had been widely circulated. Therefore, the title was thoroughly investigated during the summer of 1905 and the warranty deed and the abstract were taken before the Committee of Lumber and Mining at the legislature in Madison, and declared perfect. After a long list of transfers, dating from 1867, the abstract which my mother still holds to this day, reads:

*"The foregoing abstract made the 3rd day of October, 1900, 3 p.m. shows all instruments on file or of record in the office of the Register of Deeds in the County of Sawyer, state of Wisconsin, effecting or relating to the title of the within described land lying and being in said county.*

*"There are no unsatisfied judgements entered against any party named in said*

*abstract in any court of record having their record in said county, which are a lien on said land, except as noted, and there are no Mechanic's Liens, Attachments, Lis Pendens, or other liens or notices entered against said land except as noted. There are no unredeemed tax sales or taxes due and unpaid against said land except as noted.*

*"Witness my hand at Hayward, Wisconsin, this day and year first above written,*

*(Sealed) Ralph Tilstad, Abstractor."*

The abstract of title showed that Hattie E. Dietz purchased the 160 acres in dispute from Jennie L. Cameron, widow of Hugh L. Cameron, who was an individual logger and owned the land on which Cameron Dam was located. This proved beyond a doubt that our title was clear to the land.

On the other hand, the forty acres held by the lumber company to secure Cameron Dam for its own, as the officials believed, had been acquired in a peculiar manner, as I understand it. The widow Cameron did not know she owned that piece of land, as the lawyer handling her affairs in that part of the county kept it concealed until the taxes had been unpaid for three years. At the expiration of that time it was "sold" for taxes to the Chippewa Lumber and Boom Company, who believed that Cameron Dam was located on that small tract. Mrs. Cameron learned through my father and mother's visit to her home to complete negotiations for the land my mother purchase from her that she had owned an additional forty acres of land recently sold for taxes. She made an investigation. Under the law, she had a right to redeem the property as she had minor heirs, but the lawyer advised her not to start litigation for the lumber company was prepared to spend thousands of dollars to retain possession of the land and Cameron Dam.

Thus the lumber company rested securely in the thought that the Dam was their own, until the survey made by Mr. Sergeant at my father's request. It must have been a bitter blow at their careful planning to find that they had gone to so much trouble to acquire a measley little forty acres lying at some distance from the Thornapple River and the coveted Dam.

During the summer of 1905 we went about our farm duties without molestation. We saw men about our farm and knew we were being watched but no men came to serve any kind of papers on my father. We did, however, resolve to sell our sheep and cease trying to raise them because so many were being poisoned. Early in the autumn we sold them to a Chicago concern, and father and the boys drove them into Winter, the little village which had sprung up nine miles from us, where they were loaded into cars and shipped to Chicago. My father received $2.50 a head for the sheep, and he had one hundred seventy five.

Then, later in the autumn, an incident happened which showed how thoroughly we had been boycotted through the efforts of the lumber company. We had about forty head of young beef, not quite enough to ship to Chicago profitably, which we killed and dressed with the expectations of selling it to the markets in the village of Winter or to other lumber camps, outside of the Chippewa Lumber and Boom Company, in the vicinity. When my father took the beef to the markets in Winter they told him frankly they couldn't buy it because they feared a boycott on other provisions purchased by the lumber company. The other lumber companies gave no excuse at all, they just turned my father away when he had hauled the beef six miles down the river on a sled. They depended on the larger lumber company to buy and ship their logs each spring, and could not afford to antagonize the Chippewa Lumber and Boom Company by dealing with its enemies. We smoked and dried and ate and gave away to the neighboring homesteaders all the beef we could, and the rest was thrown on the dump pile—about half of the two tons we had butchered going to waste. We were rewarded by the queer birds our decaying beef attracted—hawks, vultures, crows, and even eagles came to the feast.

We were more successful in disposing of other crops. We sold hay to other farmers that autumn, and supplied neighboring homesteaders with potatoes and other vegetables for their root cellars. What "garden truck" my father could raise. He seemed to be endowed with the gardening instinct noted in many men of German descent. Our potatoes were twelve inches long in many instances—our pumpkins grew to County Fair Exhibit proportions, but remained tender and sweet—a head of our cabbage would fill a dish pan—and rows upon rows of firm luscious tomatoes would turn to scarlet in the late summer sunshine.

Our house was of logs, but the inside was papered with as gaily flowered wall paper as could be found in a city home. And it would have been hard to find a table as laden with good things as the one to which we sat down three times a day. We always had plenty of money to buy the latest in farm equipment—we had the only sulky plow in the county and everything else was up to standard. Our winters were long and cold, but we had plenty of wood and good warm clothing.

Our home was reported to be barricaded but this was far from the truth, and we had many friends among the better element in the village of Winter and in the surrounding neighborhood. The Bishop family, which had been our friends at Larson's Bridge, had moved to Winter, and Miss Grace Bishop was the village postmistress, with the post office in the little general store owned by her father and mother. Whenever I went to the village, I went to her house for dinner, for Grace and I had always been friends. To my knowledge she is still the postmistress, although she married a doctor a few years ago.

Mr. C. G. O'Hair, with his family, had come into the community and taken up a homestead about four miles from us. His children were about the age of those in our family, and it was largely due to his efforts that both his family and our own were provided with schools. His children had their teacher and school in their own home just as we did.

For pets we had our dogs, and an ever increasing family of cats, several pet deer.

We enjoyed our deer thoroughly. One beautiful doe we had found as a fawn starving in the woods near Price Dam, and we had taken her home and fed her and she lived with us for three years. Her favorite napping place was on a rug in front of our organ, with her head on the pedals. We frequently found fawns whose mothers had been shot out of season or caught by wolves. Sometimes we found these timid little creatures crouched under bushes, their spotted coloring making them barely discernible in the foliage; again they would come with their peculiar blatting cry to us in the wood. When we picked them up in our arms they would faint dead away, just like a person in the grip of a deadly terror. We would carry them home, and feed them warm milk with a bottle and nipple when they came to, and ever after they would be as close to us as Mary's little lamb. We found that ordinary cow's milk was too strong for the little fellows, so we sent away for Mellon's Food, and when that was fed to them they grew and thrived. Of course they matured rapidly, like all wild animals, but for the first few weeks we had to be careful indeed that bottles and nipples were clean and sterilized, for deer are as delicate and tender as human babies.

We never kept them tied or in captivity, and they roamed about at will. We tied a red woolen cloth around Molly's neck (Molly was the one who slept with her head on the organ pedals) from which was suspended a little bell. This would warn hunters that she was a pet. The bell was often a nuisance for when we would go to look for the cows, Molly would keep playing around us until her own bell made so much noise that we couldn't hear the cow bell. I would always tell my mother to keep Molly in while I went up in the field to listen for the cows, but somehow Molly would sense that I was making a little excursion and I never got far before she came bounding along, splashing in every little puddle, running to the woods and back again to meet me, and doing all the cute little antics of a playful puppy. She loved bread, and many a time she was scolded soundly by my mother because she would place her sharp little front hoofs on the dining room table and nose about in the dishes for bread. At the end of three years she failed to return to the house, but we saw her later with a fawn in the woods. We also raised a handsome buck, who was a great pet for three years. Then, he, too, returned to his wild life.

Another doe, Lucy, was a true member of the Dietz group, and suffered a fate worse than any of the rest of us. She was about a year old, gentle and tame, when we found her one morning lying beside the dam with her throat cut! Of course, we didn't know who did it, but it seemed too bad that such a dear affectionate creature should suffer.

One of our work horses was also stabbed, but we found him in time to save his life. He was a big black animal, named Paul, and the boys found him one night when they went to close the barn for the night standing in his own stall with the front of his throat and chest stabbed with a dagger. It was just far enough from the jugular vein to keep him from dying instantly, and my father and the boys were able to cure him.

We had our school again that winter of 1905-1906 and the winter and spring passed unusually quietly. Our regular farming routine was carefully followed in the spring, and when the crops were laid by, my father gave Clarence, Leslie and myself each $25 and let us go down to Rice Lake to visit our grandparents. It was a great visit, and we enjoyed the trip tremendously, and how carefully we spent our money on fancy bits of clothing and for gifts for the ones at home.

When we returned our father and mother went to Rice Lake for a visit. While there they attended Chautauqua, and my father was asked to give a little talk from the platform, when it was learned that they were in the audience. My father gave a neat little speech and received much applause.

It seems queer that the officers did not arrest him while he was so close at hand if there were warrants out for him. It seemed all through the years that we had the trouble that the depredations would be committed in spurts, with intervals of peace and quiet. We attributed this to the fact that whoever was back of our trouble thought best to let public sentiment die out between times. Then we would suddenly find our peaceful lives disturbed by totally unexpected onslaughts.

The month of July was our busy month for cutting hay. Each day a certain section of the hay would be mowed by my father or one of the boys on a big mower, and that must be put into little hay cocks, which could be safely left out overnight. But the afternoon of each day found the whole family in the barnyard, busily engaged in putting the hay in the loft. The hay can be left out only a short time to cure, and if the weather was threatening, we had to work fast indeed to get it in the barn before the clouds gathered.

The afternoon of July 25, 1906, was our busiest day of the haying season. The whole family was in the barnyard just after lunch when one really severe skirmish, which might indeed give the name of "battle" to our controversy, occurred.

Magazine Section
Part Five

# The New York Times.

SUNDAY, OCTOBER 16, 1910

Magazine Section
Part Five

## WHY DIETZ, OUTLAW, DEFIED A STATE AND AN ARMED POSSE

**Dramatic Guerilla War Ends Long Fight Between Lumber Trust and the Owner of a Dam on Thornapple River, Wisconsin.**

92

I was driving the team hitched to the hay fork, my mother was raking up wisps of hay that fell from the wagon, Leslie and my father were in the hay mow, and Clarence was on the load of hay. The small children, Helen, 9, Stanley, 6, and John, 3, were playing about the barnyard. Suddenly a cow which had been lying in the shade, peacefully chewing her cud, arose to her feet and after gazing into the flowage for an instant, started walking toward the edge of the barnlot which bordered on the flowage.

My mother noticed the cow's queer actions and called to my father about them. My father called back that she might be hearing a bear or a porcupine, and to send one of the children to see what it was. Little Helen immediately ran over to the edge of the flowage, and looked down an embankment where we had thrown all the stones we had picked up on the farm. Instantly she came running back, crying:

"Oh, it's men with guns! It's men with guns climbing up over the rocks!"

My father climbed down from the hay mow and ran to the house, returning with his gun. We could then see the grass in the flowage (which grew high as a man's head) waving in long snake-like paths as though a party of men was beating a hasty retreat. My father, Leslie, Clarence and I stood at the edge of the flowage and looked down on the rocks and high grass below. A small clump of willows stood by itself about fifteen feet from us, and as we looked about us, my father suggested that he saw something move in the willows, but added that it might have been a bird. Clarence, unarmed, move forward to investigate, and at that moment the sound of a rifle was heard, and Clarence dropped to the ground without a sound. The next instant, a bullet whizzed past Leslie's face, so close he heard its whistling. A puff of black smoke accompanied the crack of the rifle, and when my father saw it coming from the willows, he emptied his gun into the spot where it had appeared. Then he and Leslie ran to pick up Clarence.

My mother and the children had run into the house, and I ran as fast as I could to get into the house too. But I was unable to get in, for a hailstorm of bullets were being directed at the house from the woods across the flowage. They were literally peppering the front door yard, and I crouched behind a rain barrel on the north side of the house until the firing ceased. In a few minutes all was quiet and my father and Leslie carried my brother Clarence into the house.

The bullet had ploughed a furrow through the top of Clarence's head and blood was pouring from a wound big enough to lay one's finger in. The skull was fractured, and the brain was exposed in one place. When the boy (he was just 20) was carried into the house my mother ran for the carbolic acid, the iodine and a marvellously healing salve which she herself made. With these remedies and fresh bandages twice a day, she healed the wound without the aid of a doctor. As Clarence grew better, he would sit out in the sunshine, and that, coupled with my mother's healing remedies and tender care, effected his cure. For weeks, though, he couldn't bear the sound of even a pin falling on the floor, and it was a year before he was back to his normal health.

To get back to that memorable afternoon: Our anxiety over Clarence kept us in the house for several hours, and then the farmer's instinct to make hay while the sun shone took us back to the hay field. I took Clarence's place on the load and father and Leslie and I brought in the hay before dark. But, my father and Leslie carried guns while we worked.

The little battle always reminded me of a severe thunderstorm—it came so suddenly and cleared away so quickly—the sun shone so brightly afterward, and all was so quiet it almost seemed that we could hear the sounds in the forest. We didn't seem to feel any particular fear—perhaps it was because our anxiety over Clarence's condition cast out every other feeling. We had always been a very closely united family, and an injury to one of our household was a blow to all of us.

My father didn't go near the clump of willows to see if any of his shots had hit anything or anyone either that afternoon or the following morning. However, our uncle, W. W. Dietz, former sheriff of Barron County, came in much excited and told us a man had been shot when my father fired into the willows. He brought newspapers containing the following story, originating from Ladysmith, Wisconsin: *Ladysmith News Budget,* July 27, 1906

"James Hedrington, who cares for the dams of the Mississippi River Logging Company on the Thornapple River, arrived here today from the Cameron Dam and reports that an encounter has taken place between John F. Dietz and family and a body of six militiamen, accompanied by Sheriff Gylland, of Sawyer County.

"One militiaman, whose name is unknown to Hedrington, was shot three times and Clarence Dietz, son of John Dietz, was shot in the head and fell to the ground. The militiaman, who is from Milwaukee, was shot in the hip, neck and leg. His recovery is considered doubtful. The other men are bringing him to the hospital here.

"Dr. Stephenson and a number of men and teams left early today to get the party four miles above Tupper Creek.

"Hedrington says that the shooting took place yesterday afternoon. The women of the Dietz household, says Hedrington, took part in the defense and he believes that one hundred fifty shots were fired.

"Hedrington says that John Dietz jumped onto a stump when he saw the attacking party coming, and ordered them off the place. He was some distance from the house while the militiamen were in the brush. They did not see him and Hedrington says that the firing was between the Dietz family and the militia, John being some thirty rods distant. Hedrington, who was pressed into service by Sheriff Gylland, says the militiamen are all from Milwaukee. Dietz told him before the attack, says Hedrington, that he expected to die on the farm with an empty gun in his hand."

This was the first knowledge we had that the men wore uniforms, for none of us except my little sister, Helen, had laid eyes on any of these men. Helen said they had brass buttons on their coats, but she had only a fleeting glimpse of the men and we laid her statement to an over-excited childish imagination.

The rest of us saw the grass wave, we saw a movement in the clump of willows, and we heard and saw—and at least Clarence felt, the bullets which popped around us and our home, but we never saw a living soul in the attacking party.

John Rogich, we afterward learned, was shot by my father when he fired into the willows at the sight of the smoke, the bullet going through his hip and heel, as he knelt in the bushes to aim at Clarence and Leslie. He was a foreigner, just over from Austria, and fully believed himself a militiaman when provided with the National Guard uniform.

The panic that overwhelmed the little band after their fight with my father can best be shown by the following story, concerning Rogich's wounds and tribulations, as told by him to a Hayward newspaper:

"John Rogich, the Milwaukee deputy, wounded by John Dietz, was brought to Hayward yesterday afternoon by Chairman E. Arnts, of the town of Winter. Rogich has good chances of recovery, unless complications set in. He is suffering more from the two days of privation and exposure endured than from his wounds.

"His story is that he was the only one to stand and receive fire of the Dietzes and that when he fell, he plainly heard Dietz say for his son to go down and if the ******* was still alive to kill him, chop his head off and bring it up and feed it to the hogs. It was as Clarence was coming down that he took aim and shot him he says.

"Rogich then started along for the camp and waded through the water of the Thornapple River clear up to his neck. Here he was found by his companions, who undressed him and laid him upon a stretcher, and started to carry him out forgetting to bring his clothes.

"Someone raised the cry of "Dietz is coming!" and the companions deserted him. From then on, into the next day, he wandered aimlessly through the wilderness, naked and suffering excruciatingly from his wounds and the direct privations until he came upon the camp of two assessors who cared for him and brought him out to Winter.

"Great indignation is expressed here for the alleged desertion of Rogich by his companions, and taken along with their utterances upon their return to Hayward that they would not go for Dietz again if paid a thousand dollars, is in marked contrast they are reported to have expressed at their homes three hundred miles away."

A Milwaukee paper grew suspicious of the identity of the so-called militiamen for there had been no order issued by the governor. After an investigation it was learned that the five men who crept up on our farm with guns and uniforms had been hired by Sheriff Gylland of Sawyer County from the streets of Milwaukee. All were members of the National Guard, but they had no authority from headquarters to take the uniforms when they went to Sawyer County. The names of the men were William Blockowitcz, Frank Napierala, John Larose, John Rogich and John Hoeft, who hired them in Milwaukee and acted as spokesman for the group.

A short time after the incident, the following item was published in a Milwaukee paper:

> "The militiamen who wore uniforms, and assisted Sheriff Gylland of Sawyer County in his raid upon Dietz, without proper orders are to be discharged from the National Guard. It was a breach of discipline and the commander-in-chief is called upon to take immediate action."

One of interviews given by John Hoeft to a newspaper writer who sent it as a "special to the *Milwaukee Journal*" gave us a real laugh. Yes, indeed, we kept our sense of humor through it all. The story read as follows:

> "Six of the Milwaukee men who participated in the battle with John Dietz at the Cameron Dam last Wednesday returned home today. The seventh member of the party, John Rogich, who was wounded by John Dietz and his son, Charles, is in the lumber camp.
>
> "'Of the whole Dietz family,' said the leader of the party, 'I think the daughter, Myra' is the most dangerous to a sheriff bent on making an arrest. She kept firing from the time the battle began until it was over, and did not once let up except to re-load her rifle.
>
> "'She paid no attention to our shots, although, of course, we were as careful as possible not to shoot her. We were in

danger any minute of being killed by one
of her bullets. She is a corker and no
mistake.

"'If it takes a company of militia to
capture the old man, it will take a
regiment of regulars to arrest the
daughter.'"

Since I had never fired a gun in my life,
and was deathly afraid of one, we were amused
at the utter falsity of the newspaper story—
there was just as much truth to it as to the
stories that my father had been killing
deputies as fast as they stepped on the farm.
Later we had reason to believe that a sort of
alibi was being established—making the public
believe that all of us were desperate
creatures so that if I, or any of the other

innocent ones in the family, were killed, it would not seem such an outrage.

We learned that Sheriff Gylland and John Hoeft made a trip to Madison to ask Governor Davidson to send the militia to capture my father. The mere fact that Governor Davidson did not see fit to send out the militia shows that he did not think John Dietz was the outlaw he was being painted and that the Sawyer County officials should be able to handle the case.

John Rogich, the man wounded by my father, narrowly escaped death when he was deserted by his frightened companions and left to wander about the woods for two days before finding shelter. Since he had been hired by the sheriff, he felt that he had damages coming, but Sheriff Gylland filed an indignant answer to his attorney's request, and Rogich received nothing more beyond his "wages" and the bills he incurred while he was under the doctor's care at Hayward.

During the wide-spread comment after the shooting affair at our home, someone asked Sheriff Gylland what he wanted, anyhow, at John Dietz' house that day! He replied that he wanted to serve a criminal warrant charging my father with attempting to shoot deputies two years before. The old story of Elliott's so called murder had thus bobbed up again! Why had the warrant not been served on my father as he visited about the county or down at Rice Lake? The reader must bear in mind that we had 300,000 feet of timber belonging to the lumber company on our land, and it could not be touched by even a millionaire corporation unless a settlement was made with my father. The value of this timber was approximately

$10,000, and that was reason enough to want a farmer and his family off the land. It was a queer coincidence that a foreman of the lumber company should have accompanied the sheriff and his posse to our farm that July day.

We had many visitors at our log home in the days following the shooting of Clarence, but none more thoroughly enjoyed than two reporters from the *Milwaukee Journal,* whom we knew as Mr. Traynor and Mr. Rowland. The story of their experience in visiting us may best be told in their own words:

"'I want you two fellows to have a talk with this man, Dietz, at Cameron Dam. I want some pictures, too. Leave tonight and be sure not to get shot. A dead man's not worth much to a newspaper. If you fall down on this you needn't bother to come back.'

"This was about all our managing editor had to say to us, after the first fitful dispatches concerning the row on the Thornapple River began to come over the wire. We were even surprised that he had spoken at this length. Instructions from across the hall are usually terse and very much to the point. And because of this, they are not often ignored.

"Now in the first place we didn't want to see John Dietz. We thought he could get along very nicely and was at that time doing as well as could be expected of any man. We didn't know anything about his fight, and we cared still less, and we would have told him as much—over the long distance telephone!

"In the second place, it was Saturday and there are always so many things to keep a man in the city on Saturdays. We didn't object, though. We just grinned and said we would go.

"When we struck Winter, the following Monday morning the gossip of the leading citizens was not calculated to relieve our anxiety. They spoke of John Dietz as a man who shot on sight; who could pick off newspaper reporters at three hundred rods, a hundred and ninety-eight times out of two hundred shots. They said he just loved to kill people and that he was a bad, bad man. The affable gent who pushes drinks across the bar to Winter's male population told us on the quiet that Dietz salted his victims and ate them during the off-season on deer. As it was late in the day, and the distance to Dietz' clearing is twelve miles, over an uncertain trail, we decided to postpone our enterprise until the morrow. Although we knew death lurked for us somewhere in the hours between noon and nightfall, we were not sorry when the first sun of the morning broke through the window.

"With a decrepit wagon and team of lumber horses, we started for Dietz clearing. Just as we were leaving town we heard a blood-curdling shriek up the boulevard and looked up to see a be-overalled citizen sprinting in our direction with an axe in his hand. At this unfortunate moment our team balked and we decided to do battle on the spot. We thought our finish had come, but when the man reached us, he lowered his weapon and with the rarest courtesy said:

"'Thought you boys might need this 'ere axe. The roads purty bad a spell farther in!'

"We took his axe with some doubt, but discovered later that if he had presented us with a few sticks of dynamite and a saw mill our progress through the woods might have been accelerated.

"For two miles into the timber, the trail was beautiful, being not much rougher than eighteen year old cedar block pavement. Presently, however, the topography of the country changed. Boulders began to appear in the road and we found our wheels sinking deeper and deeper into the mud as we advanced. Here and there we came to big logs lying directly across the path. It was probably in this country that the man who invented the "Bump the Bumps" got his idea.

"Suddenly we came to a windfall which necessitated a flank-movement. Our forest balloon swerved just in time to keep the wheels intact and then we brought up into a natural trap made of fallen tree trunks and growing saplings. It was here that our driver said something about the axe.

"'Someone's got ter do some almighty choppin' about now!' he vouchsafed without much interest, implying that his duties began and ended in the role of driving. The other fellow had regaled us with stories of his adventures when he had been a woodsman of no mean reputation, during the long hours already consumed in our drive, and personally, I believed that here was a splendid opportunity for him to make good. A man who knew so much about signs in the forest, and animals, as he, surely would have little difficulty with a wee sapling. He made no move, however, and so I took the axe and did the chopping.

"It was about that time the other fellow happened to get a glimpse of a porcupine crossing the road.

"'A wild animal! Get him! Get him!' he yelled as he jumped from the wagon and ran after the poor little creature tugging a little revolver from his pocket.

"I was out of the wagon in a moment with my trusty axe. The other fellow saw my weapon and turned on me an eye of scorn. 'Aren't you dead game sport,' he remarked bitingly. 'You ought to do your hunting with a pile driver.'

"I could not stand the contumely and dropped the axe shamefacedly in the brush. Then I got my own revolver and the two of us gave chase. The porcupine saw us coming and made for a tall tree. He went up like a lineman on a telegraph pole and we tacked on two feet behind him. When the three of us got to the top, the other fellow and I opened up with our revolvers. Mr. Porcupine sat up on a limb and looked around curiously and the bullets whizzed around his head. After we had expended our ammunition we climbed down again, leaving our friend swinging unconcernedly from a bough.

"If I'd had the axe I'll bet I'd a' got him.

"Along about now I came to the conclusions the other reporter's experiences in wood lore had been confined to Lake and Washington Parks.

"When we climbed into the wagon again the driver told us he could go no farther. From the looks of the road ahead we judged he was speaking the truth, so there was nothing left but to walk the remainder of the distance.

"'You'd better let me take keer o' them guns,' he advised. 'Why, ef John Dietz saw them cap pistols he prob'ly would confiscate 'em for the baby to teeth on.'

"His observation was good, we thought, so we stripped of every weapon with the exception of the camera. Equipped thus, we struck out over the woods. We travelled thus for miles, ready at any moment and at the slightest sound to dive under the nearest bush. Then without warning we plunged abruptly into an opening in the trees at the edge of a river.

"A log cabin stood on a hillside across the stream and cattle were grazing in a pasture. We were at Cameron Dam.

"Our plans had been to march boldly up to the river, wading across and continuing to the house as though we owned the place. The situation had now involved itself into who was to take the lead. I thought perhaps the other fellow would go first and he sort of held back to see what I was going to do. There was nothing for it then but to walk abreast. We held our hands conspicuously from our pockets and made the great advance.

"Up until now we had seen no one, but as we looked towards the house a head emerged from the back door and the front end of a champion piece of all the heavy ordinances we had ever seen was pushed through the opening. A man's body followed and we knew him for John Dietz. He came down to the bank to greet us and then we perceived that he was carrying a gun bigger than we had first supposed.

"'Lookin' for somebody?' he inquired pointedly.

"'No, we're not lookin' for anyone—that is, we would like—if you are Mister John Dietz ... why ....'

"'Say, what do you want anyhow?' And the gun was moved slightly in one direction and we hoped it would not point.

"'Hello, Mister Dietz, we know it is you, now!" We shouted playfully. 'We're only two newspaper reporters and do not intend to capture you!'

"'Gwan, quit your crowdin' behind me,' I said in an undertone to the other fellow. 'Do you think I want to be the only one that gets shot?'

"'Come on over', said Dietz, grinning, evidently satisfied that we were harmless. In another moment we had forged the river and we were on the famous farm.

"Before we had been there ten minutes we had decided that John Dietz was a gentleman. After a while he put away his gun in order to do the honors of the place with better grace. The dinner he gave us was a thing of joy forever. After our walk and our relief that we were not to be shot as per schedule, we could have eaten anything. When Mrs. Dietz put a pot of stew on the table and our friend John told us to fall to—we fell. Our trip convinced us of one thing—that the Dietzes were not likely to be starved out at least.

"What manner of man is John Dietz? What is the life led by his family on the lonely banks of the Thornapple River? Is the famous Cameron Dam outlaw of the same type as Jesse James, Tracy,—notorious fighting men and killers?

"These are among the questions that have recently come to the people of Wisconsin—questions that cannot be answered even by the former friends of the sturdy settler. The terrible successes of the game fighter who has pitted himself, single-handed, against corporations, has made him a man not of the twentieth century. To the neighbors who used to know him before he became a fugitive of justice, John Dietz has become a character in a thrilling book of romance. His exploits have made him a man apart, and although the sympathies of Sawyer County are with him, the residents fear him and shun him and speak of him with awe, forgetting the time when he had a place in the midst of them.

"John Dietz is of German extraction—a man in the prime of life, about five-feet ten inches in height, wiry and active. His complexion is ruddy and his hair and moustache are sandy in color. He is a skilled woodsman, a shrewd politician, a reader of standard literature and a good shot with rifle and revolver. He is a Mason of many years standing, having at one time occupied a prominent position in the Rice Lake Lodge, in which town he held the office of Justice of the Peace.

"To one who approaches him as a friend, Dietz is not the terrible fighting man, pictured by the residents of the district. His face, frank and open, is seared with lines of irrepressible good spirits. His blue eyes sparkle with humor. His mouth is expressive and almost tender. This is the John Dietz who welcomed the representatives of the *Journal*.

"The enemies of Dietz, however, describe an entirely different personage. When he is aroused the human eyes narrow to a pair of slits, cold and repellent. The lines of humor give way to deeper ones of determination and hatred. The mouth straightens and compresses until it is like a scar left by the lash of a saber. This is the other John Dietz— terror to sheriffs and posses, the fugitive.

"'I am the poet laureate of Thornapple River', he remarked with a grin. I haven't any rivals or competitors or critics to contend with, and the admirers of my works are restricted to seven persons, my family. I don't believe my poetry will ever become very popular, I tried it once on an outsider,' he finished with a chuckle.

"'It was a poem I had written about
Sheriff Gylland:
'See the mighty host advancing,
Gylland leading on,
Mighty men and heroes falling,
Courage almost gone

Hold the fort, for I am coming,
With my pepper gun;
Watch the smoke, watch the shooting,
Watch the Sheriff run!'

"'You may think I am getting too
humorous,' he said apologetically. 'It is
so seldom that I have a chance to
exchange courtesies with outsiders, that
when I do find a friend I immediately
make him my enemy by talking him to
death. Lets not talk about my troubles—I
always lose my temper and then I am not
pleasant company. What's doing
politically outside in the state—maybe we
can get into a little argument?'
"With his family of seven, Dietz has
made himself a wonderful home in the
forest. He has cleared one hundred sixty
acres of land, all of which is under
cultivation, feeds a herd of several cows
and sheep and a large flock of poultry.
His famous cabin is built on the crown of
a hill, commanding a clear sweep of
country for two hundred yards on all
sides. A little spring of sweet water
bubbles at the foot of this hill,
attracting thirsty deer from the forest.
He is able to kill these animals from the
back door of his cabin.

"To drive a wagon through the woods to Cameron Dam is an impossibility, the little clearing being surrounded on all sides by almost impenetrable forest. A lumber road at one time led from Winter straight to Dietz clearing, but this trail has long since become choked with logs and windfalls. Yet with all its drawbacks, Dietz says he loves his farm and could remain contented there if he was free from molestation.

"Miss Almira Dietz, 'the girl who can shoot like a man', is above all things a woman. She is the one member of the outlawed family who is not quite contented with her lot. Her pride and love for her father, however, will not permit her to complain.

"'I am with him through it all,' she said simply. 'If death awaits at the end, I can ask nothing better than to go with my father and brothers.'

"'People think I am an Amazon,' she declared. 'I have never fired a shot in anger. The day may come when it may become necessary for me to use my rifle in defense of my home, though. When I am forced to that, I think I can provide good measure.'

"In the meantime, Miss Dietz follows the pursuits of a farmer's daughter. Her recreations are simple. She possesses an excellent contralto voice and she plays unusually well on an organ which her father brought over the trail on a sled a number of years ago.

"In the long evenings, assessors and others who have been overtaken by the

night and forced to pitch a tent near the
Dietz clearing, have been startled upon
hearing the notes of a little forgotten
love song, floating across the clearing
into the woods. It is the voice of Almira
Dietz, the girl who has never had a
lover, and who does not herself know she
is calling to the man who only exists in
her dreams—who may never come to her.
Miss Dietz longs to be as other girls.
She has talent for drawing and would go
to school if she could. The interior of
the little cabin is decorated with her
work—copies from all magazines, the deer
drinking from the spring—in the whole
collection is not a portrayal of shooting
and bloodshed.

"The mother of the family, Mrs. Hattie
Dietz, is happy with her children. At one
time a school mistress, Mrs. Dietz has
expanded infinite pains upon the
education of her boys and girls. Upon a
table in the living room of the cabin is
a stack of dog-eared text books, even
Clarence, the oldest boy, and Johnny
'Ginger', Jr., the youngest, are not
exempt from discipline, being forced to
devote a certain period of each day to
their studies.

"'I cannot bring myself to believe
that the end of it all will be a
tragedy,' Mrs. Dietz said. 'Everything is
so beautiful and so green in the woods
and the very song of the birds renews my
hope that all is bound to come out right
in the end. A mother cannot predict
defeat for her children, no matter what
the prospects. It is too much to expect.

We are giving them what education we can with the hope that someday they may become good and useful citizens.'

"Not because he has been shot and is a man in daring and fighting prowess, if not in year, but because he is a master in woodcraft, a leader in boyish sports, Clarence, the oldest son, is a wonderful hero to his brothers and sisters. Because he has no companions of his own age, he has adjusted to fit the appreciation of his younger relatives, permitting them to participate in his games.

"In the winter it is Clarence who builds the slide from the cabin down to the river brink, who makes the sleds and the snow forts and who can cut his own name in the ice with skates. Again it is Clarence who can pitch curves with a baseball. He can run like a deer, knock squirrels from the tall trees with his rifle and perform many feats in the water. The younger children are proud of Clarence.

"As a family, the Dietzes are happy. They have their home, the forest, the river and their simple pleasures. The life they hav lead has made them strong and robust, and the mutual, constant danger has drawn the ties closer and closer until their understanding of one another is perfect. Dietz has expressed his position, at the same time accounting for the great fight he has made, when he said: 'I care for nothing in the world but my family and my home, and I shall never give up, either.'"

Sheriff James Gylland

As a result of the interviews of the two "Journal Scribes" appearing in the *Milwaukee Journal*, our home was flooded with expressions of sympathy from all over the country. Reporters from the *Superior Telegram*, *Fond du Lac Bulletin*, *St. Paul Dispatch*, *Minneapolis Tribune*, *New York World*, *Chicago Tribune*, *Milwaukee Sentinel*, *Madison Journal* and many other large papers came to get our story. It seemed that practically all the small town papers in the state were represented by their editors, who came in person to see and hear our unusual family.

The *Journal* stories were the first authentic reports to go out—it was the first time our side of the controversy had been given to the public. And it seemed that the great American public was with us, to a man! Petitions were signed in hundreds of cities and town asking Governor Davidson to investigate our case and take some action to make life safe for the Dietz family. He was urged to quash any indictments against us if they were found to be illegal, and allow us to live like any other American family.

Governor Davidson remained solidly on the fence throughout the entire matter. His reply to one suggestion was typical of his attitude throughout the controversy. The following was taken from the *Milwaukee Journal* when public sentiment was at its height:

"Alderman Henry Smith, who suggested to Governor Davidson that he call upon John Dietz in person and say, 'Here, Neighbor, what's the matter? Let's see if we cannot settle this!' has received the following letter from the Governor's private secretary, Col. O. G. Munson:

"'Yours of recent date relating to the attempted arrest of John Dietz is at hand. I am directed by the governor to advise you that he has taken no action whatever in the matter.

"'Some months ago application was made by the Sheriff of Sawyer County for the aid of the Wisconsin National Guard for the arrest of Mr. Dietz, and the Governor did not then feel justified, upon the information at hand, to grant the request. Should a further application be made by the sheriff the matter will receive careful investigation.

"'Governor Davidson thanks you for your kindly suggestions concerning the matter.'"

The columns of the *Milwaukee Journal* were thrown open for expressions of its readers on the Dietz case and literally thousands of them were received, among which were the following:

"Dietz is harming no one, he simply protects his property, himself and his family. Must he do what the logging company says? And, if not, will they arrest him? Is that the law? The law should protect the poor as well as the rich."

"I think Wisconsin should be proud that they have one man, or man and family, like Dietz, able to defy authorities who are trying to help defraud him of his rights and not give him a just compensation for labor performed."

"I am surprised that the fair city of Milwaukee had so cowardly and mean a class of men as the two or three which went to Cameron Dam to capture such a brave man as John Dietz, who is merely fighting for his rights and the rights of his wife and children. It is the duty of every loyal citizen in the country to protect such a man. All that is to be regretted is that he didn't kill that cowardly Rogich and Hoeft. One man like Dietz is worth more to this country than a hundred thousand of them."

"Sawyer County ought not to allow the disgrace of a tragedy when a few dollars will prevent it. The example of patriotism, of mother and children, for father and home, is worth more to the state than all the logs that can be floated down the Thornapple River in a century. If the time ever comes that Dietz is dangerous to the community let the state exert her authority and take him dead or alive—but not now—too great a sacrifice for the gain."

"My opinion of the Dietz case is that Mr. Dietz is right in defending himself and his home. If he surrendered he wouldn't get a fair trial, as the lumber company has more money than he and money talks. I think everyone should help Mr. Dietz fight for his freedom."

"Dietz did perfectly right by shooting Rogich, who was trying his best to shoot Dietz' wife and children. I only wish he would have given Sheriff Gylland a smell, as he really deserved it. I think if Gylland will make another attempt to capture Dietz he will get all he is looking for."

"I think Mr. Dietz has been shamefully treated by the lumber company and he should be paid."

"We think John Dietz a very brave man to protect his family and home and I don't see why Governor Davidson doesn't make that logging company settle properly with John Dietz. Feeling is running high around here in favor of Dietz. We don't think for a minute that John Dietz is an outlaw, as Davidson so often called him."

"Have Governor Davidson send his troops and make the lumber company pay John F. Dietz what they owe him. Because they are a wealthy corporation is no reason why they can make a man with the courage that Mr. Dietz has shown forgive them a debt and simply move away and make them a present of all he possesses. John Dietz wasn't built that way. I, for one, uphold him in his action and I should say for courage and the bravery shown by him, he ought to get a medal."

"In regard to the John Dietz case, I would say that I think the lumber company should pay him in full for his work and that sheriff and hirelings of any sort should keep away from him. I would add that opinion is nearly unanimous among the sturdy burghers of our town."

"If Dietz had been paid by the lumber company long ago, few people outside of his own county would have known of his existence. Northern Wisconsin would not have been Russianized by calling forth a band of Cossacks under pretense of upholding the law, but in reality to murder an innocent family for no other reason than that they were paid to do it. This is evidenced by the fact that they repeatedly fired into the house when Dietz whom they were after was acknowledged by themselves to be thirty rods from it and in clear view. If there is any prosecution, prosecute the real offenders and not John Dietz. I have talked with and heard a great many men express their views and have yet to hear the first one condemn Dietz."

"Dietz is a man worthy of praise for his courage in protecting his wife, his family and his property. If half the men of our country were half as courageous and good-natured as he is, then this certainly would be a strong and fearless country. Let us stand up for special privileges to none, not even the rich lumberman."

"Had Governor Davidson sent troops to defend Dietz against such outrageous treatment as he has had, he would have

shown himself more of a man. I think when
Governor Davidson calls people outlaws
and criminals he had better lay his false
names where they so justly belong. I hope
if they molest Dietz any more his
ammunition will hold out and he will make
good aim."

"In the recent battle, why did Sheriff
Gylland fly from his post as commanding
officer under the pretense of obtaining
medicine for the wounded, when according
to the rules of war, a high private
should have been detailed for that duty?"

"My views concerning Dietz are that
Dietz should be severely left alone or
valid cause for proceedings shown. Sham
prosecutions amount to persecutions.

"I say that the people of Wisconsin
should ask Governor Davidson to send the
National Guards to the Dietz fort at
Cameron Dam to help John F. Dietz defend
and protect the property and lives of an
honest, peaceful family against the hired
men of that corporation."

"Let Dietz alone. I was born and
raised neighbors to the Dietz family and
I have known the family all my life. I
must say I have never known anything but
good of the family, as Mr. Dietz and wife
have always been the first to lend a
helping hand to anyone in need."

"I should say the Governor Davidson
should go to Sawyer County and give John

Dietz immunity and make the logging company pay what is justly due him. This is the sentiment of ninety-five per cent of the people in northern Wisconsin. I think the people of the state of Wisconsin ought to give John Dietz about three terms in the United States Senate. I think he would be a great man to help curb corporations. He is only doing what every honest man ought to give him credit for, and what he has been driven to do."

"Let the people put up a monument as high as they can get it for the man who has the grit to stand up for his rights against the millionaire. If John Dietz is an outlaw, tell me, editor, what are those he's fighting against? My sympathy is with John Dietz."

"The man who goes into the woods and clears a farm and makes it produce good fruit and grain without means or money and raises a family comfortably as well, that man is a grand success. And John Dietz has done all this, things have come to a pretty pass when thugs can be hired to go into the woods and murder him."

"A few people choose to call Dietz an outlaw—and why? Simply because he has stamina enough to protect his rights, his property and his family, as any American citizen should!"

"The only trouble is that both he and his plucky daughter did not shoot oftener and more accurately."

"The authorities should not stand pat and look at a hungering corporation turning their hirelings loose until they drive the man and every member of his family insane by the anxiety and worry of tending his crops with his gun on his back in order to be safe from the howling mob."

"I think Governor Davidson did right not to send armed forces to Cameron Dam to slaughter Dietz and his family, but should send the militia if need be to guard and protect the settler against a gang of ruffians. Dietz is fighting in his own defense and protecting his own property and family, which every honest man has a right to do. Let Dietz alone and he will harm no one."

Sawyer County did not hesitate to express its opinion as well, despite the fact that it was Sawyer County officials who were giving up so much trouble. Here is one expression, printed in the *Milwaukee Journal*:

"Officers, away from Dietz! In my opinion, John Dietz is in the right and that is the belief of at least ninety-five per cent of the people in Sawyer County. The Governor of Wisconsin ought to send troops to protect John Dietz and his family. If there is any man who would like to capture Dietz, the farmer ought to put a bullet through his nose and say: Leave me alone, and keep your nose out of my business!"

We had never backed down for an instant in our thought that we should protect our home from the logging interests, but naturally, we were delighted to know that so great a majority of "outsiders" upheld us in our claim.

We held a continual 'reception' in our home in those days. Writers, and prominent men from many other states as well as from Wisconsin, came to see us. They usually came in the morning and would stay all day. This meant company meals every day—but it was in the summer time and we had peas, string beans, lettuce and plenty of other garden truck. Then of course we had plenty of cream, milk and butter, and hundreds of chickens ready for the frying pan. Homemade bread and hot biscuits didn't hurt the meal, either, and I was proud of my ability as a cook. We fed our guests well—and the old saying that the way to a man's heart lies through his stomach might have been proved by this fact. At any rate, every writer returned to his desk a friend of John Dietz and nothing but the truth concerning the controversy was printed.

Mr. Charles Broughton, then of the *Fond du Lac Bulletin* and now the owner of the *Sheboygan Daily Press*, and Mr. A. E. Roese, of the *Osceola Sun*, now deceased, were two of the editors who came to see us at that time. From then on, they were staunch friends, ready to help us at any time. They realized during the visit the conditions which we faced. Although we could supply our table from our farm, we did not raise sufficient grain to keep our stock through the winter. Then, too, there was the boycott against our products which I have already mentioned, and we could not sell anything to provide clothing for the family. Those two keen-sighted men saw all that, and immediately after returning to their respective papers began organizing committees for relief all over the state. These committees solicited funds and clothing which were sent on to us—and how gratefully they were received!

Descriptions of our sizes were published in the various papers and it was simply miraculous the way the clothing fitted the member of the family for whom it was meant. Dresses of every description for my mother, my little sister and myself; suits of clothes for my brothers and father; warm underwear, stockings, mittens, winter coats and garments of every sort came neatly packed in huge wooden boxes. Not a thing went to waste—we were clothed for years from the contents of those boxes. The two editors gave up their own time to personally bring the boxes right to our door, hiring wagons at Winter to transport them, feeling that it would be an imposition to ask us to take one of our teams from the field to make the trip for them.

For a period of many weeks after the shooting affair, public sentiment was so strong that we were not molested. We harvested our crops in peace and quiet. Clarence was slowly convalescing under my mother's tender care. Mr. Graham, our teacher, returned to our home and school opened as usual in the little log room off the kitchen. Our home was more quiet than it had ever been, with less laughter, less romping, and fewer outbursts of song—partly because of the subdued feeling prompted by the long strain, but more because Clarence was extremely sensitive to any noise and subject to severe headaches if fatigued or nervous.

During the fair season, my mother, father and brother Leslie went to Rice Lake to spend a week with my grandparents and to attend the fair. My father and Leslie also attended the state fair at St. Paul, a distance of sixty miles from Rice Lake. They were interviewed by reporters and the story was again published that my father had no intention of giving up his farm, come what might!

After their return from the fair, my father and brothers built an additional sleeping room to the home. We were often asked to accommodate hunters for the night, but our own family had outgrown our cabin so we felt that another room was needed to take care of guests. We needed the money, too, for times were hard, and hunters, appreciating our good food, were generous pay! My father and the boys cut the logs from our own farm, and hewed them to make the walls smooth to be papered or whitewashed. A good floor was put in, and six bunks, in regular boat fashion, were constructed against the walls. The middle of the room was given over to a big stove, table and chairs. It was clean and attractive.

The room was not built in vain. Due to the publicity we had received, our farm became more popular than ever for hunters, and the new room was seldom empty. And for the first time, many wives accompanied their huntsman husbands, seizing the opportunity to visit us when their husbands came to hunt.

My father and brothers scouted for the hunters and did a little hunting on their own account. In this manner they were able to show our appreciation for what Mr. Broughton and

Mr. Roese had done for us. Mrs. Broughton was presented with two choice otter skins, hand plucked, and tanned ready to be made into a handsome fur neckpiece. Mrs. Roese was presented with a magnificent bear skin for a rug.

My father had a strict set of rules which proved of value to more than one hunter. These rules concerned the confusion and the worry resulting from "being lost" in the woods. All of the hunters, of course, were unaccustomed to the woods, and it was no uncommon thing for a man to become lost in the dense timber on our farm, and on the farms adjoining. My father made it quite clear that once "lost" the hunter should sit quietly in one place until supper time—then if he had not appeared to eat it would be known at the house that he was lost and a lookout would be maintained for him. At dusk, then, the lost hunter should fire one shot, followed after a short interval by two more shots in rapid succession. These would be answered from our house, and the hunter should remain seated in one place, firing his rifle occasionally, while my father and the other huntsmen took lanterns and went to get him. The edict to remain in one place was strongly impressed upon the hunters for a lost man wanders about in circles, and he might be wandering vaguely about in great rings while the searching party was looking for him. Then, too, swamps and dangerous places lay in the woods and the lost man might wander into them in his confusion. Many an evening we had to keep food warm while my father and the boys went out and brought in a hungry huntsman to a belated supper.

Thus the winter of 1906-1907 passed. My father and mother celebrated their Silver Anniversary on February 9, 1907. They received many gifts from all over the state and many letters and cards of congratulation. Mr. Michigan Elliott, who had corresponded with my father for several months, was visiting at our home at that time, so he was the only guest. He was a painter and contractor at Sussex, Wisconsin, and on his way home he stopped at Milwaukee and disposed of my father's stock of furs which he had acquired during the winter. Among them were a silver gray fox, for which my father received $500, and two otter skins which brought $50 each. With the bounty on the wolf skins, and the sale of the pelts, his total fur check ran about $700.

We put in our crops as usual when spring came. Clarence was almost well again and the farm work went on as in previous years. The pile of logs still remained on our farm where they had been washed when the dam was blown out, but the specified time of three years was drawing to a close. Thus at the beginning of the month of May, 1907, we made preparations to advertise them in two county papers and post the notice of the sale of the logs on a public thoroughfare, as required by law. The advertisements were printed for several successive weeks, and the notice was duly posted—but when the day of the sale dawned not one person attended to bid on the logs. But at the appointed hour, our whole family and the school teacher went down to the log pile and my mother, who was the owner of the farm and legally the possessor of the logs, put them up for sale by reading the legal document drawn up for such occasions. We all bid spiritedly,

the school teacher and all of us, but my
father's bid was highest and he became the
owner of the logs. We did not saw them until
the following year, however, allowing them to
lie undisturbed for another season.

About the time of the sale of the logs, two
other events having an important bearing on
our case were happening. One of these was an
investigation by the Grand Jury which resulted
in the following findings:

"We, the Grand Jury of Sawyer County,
present here-with three indictments
against John F. Dietz, one for resisting
an officer and two for attempted murder.

"We think it proper to further report
that a part of the county at Cameron Dam
on Thornapple River is not subject to the
laws of the state and had not been for
three years, but has been held by John F.
Dietz, by armed force in defiance of law
and in contempt of the court.

"Property of great value is withheld
from its owners and officers and citizens
have been fired upon and their lives
endangered.

"We have examined the county records
and find that in the year of 1900 Dietz
bought 160 acres of land from Jennie
Cameron, taking the title out in his
wife's name. In 1877 the Daniel Shaw
Company built a dam on the corner of the
land in question under charter from the
state and on February 2, 1875, purchased
from Barrows and Levitt, who had owned it,
and the land and perpetual right to
maintain and operate the dam. In the year
1883, heirs of Daniel Shaw sold the dam

and all their rights to the present owners. For more than twenty-five years the dam was used for log driving purposes, without any claim of ownership being made.

"Some time after Dietz bought the land he took possession of the land and all the logs in the river about it and holds them, claiming several thousands of dollars for tolls. The owner of the logs have used all peaceable means to get their property. They have tried law and arbitration but Dietz will not recognize the courts and refuses to arbitrate on any terms. It appears that the log owners have been compelled to abandon their property.

"Four criminal warrants have been regularly issued against Dietz. The first was sworn out by John Mulligan, on a charge of assault and battery; the second by Patrick Magin for attempted murder; the third by the District Attorney for the same offense, and the fourth by James Gylland, also for attempted murder.

"Different bodies of officers have done everything that can reasonably be expected of them, but owing to the location of the place, and the character of the surrounding country, it seems impossible for any civil officer to arrest him without loss of life.

"There is reason to believe that he is more or less insane, or at least desperate. A military force will be necessary to take him if blood-shed is to be avoided.

"We think that the state should take the matter in hand and use sufficient force to arrest him, if possible, without the loss of life, as it may turn out that he is not mentally responsible.

"Representing the law-abiding people of this county, we regret that any man is permitted to defy our courts and shoot down our officers. Such things bring the law into contempt and encourage secret and open enemies of orderly government.

"We, therefore, recommend that inasmuch as it seems impossible for the county officers to put an end to anarchy that exists at Cameron Dam, the governor again be requested to take the matter in charge and restore the authority of the courts throughout this county."

The other event was the Weber Bill introduced in the legislature by Mr. Frank J. Weber, of Milwaukee, asking an investigation and report on the merits of the case against my father. After a heated discussion, during which it was brought out that a dangerous precedent would be established and the rights of the courts slighted, the bill was defeated.

After the grand Jury's report had been made, and the indictments returned the newspapers began to wonder who would serve the warrants! Sheriff Clark, who had been elected at the past election, got his name in the papers when he began summoning a posse of one hundred men with the avowed intention of taking my father. He deputized about fifty of the prominent business men and leading citizens of Hayward and as many more from the surrounding country, and arranged a meeting at a specified time and place to lay the plans for my father's capture. Only thirty of the men appeared at the meeting but many plans were discussed, none of which materialized for a period of three years.

The summer of 1907 passed peacefully. We harvested our crops and put in our hay without any trouble from any source. Nothing was done during that time relative to the grand jury's investigation, and somehow we felt more free and easy than in many months. We went to the village of Winter regularly and to church every Sunday, and mingled as usual with a few select friends. But we were not allowed to go about the country much—whether because my father feared for our safety or because he wished to rear us carefully, I cannot say. I remember one Sunday we went to church and were than coaxed by the Larson family to go down to Larson's bridge for the day and return to the evening services before going home. We allowed ourselves to be persuaded, and were going home through the woods with the driving team about nine-thirty that night when we saw a light approaching. It proved to be my father, carrying a lantern, and going to meet us or look for us. My mother was nervous and worried when we reached the house, and we were a most contrite trio.

Sherburn M. Becker, known as the "Boy Mayor" of Milwaukee, visited us in September, 1907, staying overnight with us. We enjoyed his visit, for he came in clad in a lumberman's costume with the typical corduroy shirt, driver's boots and slouch hat and made himself very much at home. He must have enjoyed his visit with us, too, for he wrote glowing accounts of my father's friendly, pleasing manner and made it thoroughly understood that he was quite in sympathy with the Dietz family in our controversy with the lumber company. When he came in to see us he brought a great number of magazines and a large quantity of candy, which won our hearts immediately. After his return to Milwaukee he sent many gifts to us, among them a pair of skates for myself. He learned during his visit that I had no skates of my own, but used the boys' which meant wearing heavy shoes and several pair of socks making my feet heavy and clumsy. He sent me the shiniest, brightest, sharpest pair of skates I'd ever seen.

Winter came with the usual rush that year, and while the farmers might have wished for its delay, the lumber company was ready for it. At great cost, as mentioned before, a railroad had been constructed from Thornapple River across the wooded country to the Flambeau River.

Then with the aid of a steam log hauler, the logs were skidded over the snow from the places along the river bank where they had been flung by the torrent at the time the dam went out in May, 1904. Of course, they could not touch the 300,000 feet of logs which still lay uncut on my mother's farm, without making a settlement with her, or with my father who had bought them at the legally authorized auction the previous summer. These logs, however, constituted only one tenth of the total cutting of timber which they were attempting to float down the Thornapple River at the time the dam was blown out, and the remaining nine-tenths lay scattered far and near along the banks of the river both above and below our farm at Cameron Dam. Newspaper reports told of the logging operations and stated that when the last of the logs had been skidded out the company would have ended their controversy with my father as the company would have no further use for Cameron Dam.

Mr. W. E. Moses, of Northfield, Minnesota, had the contract for hauling the logs to the Flambeau River for the Mississippi River Logging Company, the name now used by our old enemy, the Chippewa Lumber and Boom Company. As soon as Mr. Moses came into the vicinity, he came direct to our house, on, what he called, a "personal visit to talk things over". My father recited our wrongs at the hands of the lumber company, stating that our first trouble began with them through their refusal to pay him three years' wages earned at Price Dam. Mr. Moses said:

"Mr. Dietz, I'll get that for you."

We had heard wild promises before, and took little stock in this one, I must admit, but a week later Mr. Moses returned to the house with a roll of bills for my father. The amount was $1717.00, the full amount with interest due my father for his services as watchman at Price Dam for three years.

Mr. Moses was a man of charming personality—and he certainly won the hearts of all of us with his kind and generous spirit. We knew he was working for the interests of the lumber company, but somehow, we felt that he was in sympathy with us, and his kindness to us in later years bore out that supposition. When he gave the money to my father, he said:

"Now, Mr. Dietz, what will you take to settle in full with the lumber company? Just what will you take to walk right out of here with your family and hereafter when anyone asks how you settled with the lumber company, just say absolutely nothing!"

How angry that made my father:

"What?" he shouted. "Do you mean to say that after the company has tried to murder my family, I should go away and say nothing? No, indeed! We'll fight to the end right here!"

Mr. Moses still sat with the roll of bills in his hand, and as he talked to my father, he flaunted the bills about, idly flipping them out in long rows as a sleight-of-hand performer deftly wields a deck of cards on the vaudeville stage. Evidently, he believed that the sight of so much money would immediately swerve the Dietz family from any decision they might have made.

But my father was not to be swerved! Despite Mr. Moses' excellent orations on the value of good educations for the children, a home in some pleasant friendly village, and other alluring features which he dangled before my father's eyes, the decision to fight to the end was not changed!

Clarence, Leslie and I begged my father to accept the offer of the lumber company, and move out with us! We begged him to take a long trip, perhaps in Canada among strangers who knew nothing of the trouble, and return at the end of a year or so to take up his home elsewhere. Perhaps my father might have done as we asked, but there was one condition in the terms of settlement which my father could not and would not accept. That required him to sign a contract with the lumber company and enter their employ! How my father raged at that clause in the offer!

"I couldn't turn traitor to all the people who have sympathized with me in my fight with the lumber company," he said.

"I could never enter the employ of a company which I have fought so long and steadily. They would probably want me to steal from or murder some other poor fellow who is fighting for his rights! I can't give up my principles for money, no matter how much!"

Mr. Moses finally gave up and after leaving us the $1717.00 went about his work removing the logs strewn above and below our farm.

Although my father so flatly refused to accept the terms of the lumber company, the report that he had settled for $15,000.00 was widely broadcast. Literally hundreds of newspapers printed the story—and letters of congratulations were printed editorially and sent to my father. We tried to deny the reports but my father's feeble protestations of denial could not stop the flood of snappily written stories under headlines such as "DIETZ WINS OUT", "DIETZ WINS HIS GREAT FIGHT OVER THE RIGHT TO THORNAPPLEI DAM", "COMPANY PAYS DIETZ $15,000 AND WILL RUN THE LOGS", "DIETZ WINS THE BIG FIGHT AND $15,000 IS HIS PRIZE", "DIETZ WINS FROM THE LUMBER COMPANY AND IS ENTITLED TO A GOLD MEDAL", "LUMBER COMPANY HAS SURRENDERED TO DIETZ", and "HAS HELD THE FORT FOR THREE YEARS AND WINS".

Thus the public was given the impression that all hostilities between the lumber company and my father were ended. He had been paid liberally, according to the stories, and held no malice against the lumber company for what had been done. But the stories were far from true! The settlement for $1717 had nothing whatever to do with our situation.

When my father's denials began to seep into the press, we had another rash of visitors seeking the true story. Among these was Mr. L.

B. Nagler, chief clerk in the office of the secretary of state. Mr. Nagler became our good friend and wrote many newspaper articles in our favor, lauding my father's kindness, shrewdness and his firm adherence to his principles. He also said many nice things of the other members of the family, for which we are still grateful. He discussed the matter of our title, which had been questioned, and made it quite plain that my mother's title to the farm was perfect. Being a lawyer, and the editor of a prominent paper before going to Madison, he was thoroughly equipped to make a study of the title and put his findings into words that the public could understand. Never again was the title questioned.

The problem of keeping our valuable papers and the roll of bills received from Mr. Moses was no small matter in a farm home far from the bank or any other safety deposit vault. Our papers were kept in the back of our parlor organ. When my father would say "Get the papers", for practically all visitors wanted to see the title to our farm, one of us would go into the room where the organ stood and after closing the door carefully, we would remove the back of the organ, and take out our treasured papers. The matter of the $1717 was something more difficult—but we did what many other families have done with their treasures in times of stress—we buried the money! A little stump stood beside the pathway which led to a small elevation known in the family as "The Mountain Peak". There, under the little stump, one bright day in the late autumn, the precious money was buried in a tight tin box. Everyone in the family knew where it was buried, so if anything happened to us, those who were left would know where to look for the family fortune.

Mr. Gates returned for his third term of school in that winter of 1907-1908 and life in the cabin and school room went on as usual.

We frequently went to the lumber camp which had been constructed a mile above us, and ate dinner with the lumbermen as the guests of Mr. Moses. Then we spent glorious afternoons watching the steam log hauler making its trips to the railroad with great loads of logs. My father frequently went with us, and occasionally my mother joined the party, too. We all liked Mr. Moses, despite his connection with our bitter enemy, the lumber company, and he liked us, too. At Christmas time that year he bought my mother a beautiful set of dishes, bringing them in personally.

It was there at the logging camp, too, that we talked over a telephone for the first time in six years—excepting of course the times when we visited our grandparents at Rice Lake. Mr. Moses had had a telephone line constructed from the camp to Winter, and we thought it great fun to talk over it.

Spring came early in 1908, and the lumber company had about a million, five hundred thousand feet of logs left when the warm weather set in. It was decided to ship these to Chippewa Falls the following winter by rail. This meant that the logging activities were carried over through the winter of 1908-1909, although the report that all would be finished in 1908 had been widely circulated.

Summer was a busy time at our farm that year. My father cleared a new piece of land, blowing out the stumps and great rocks with dynamite to make it tillable. Automobiles had

become common in the county and already my
father was talking of the day when we would
own a Ford. A good county highway had been
constructed, passing about three miles from
our farm. My father and the boys undertook the
construction of the three mile stretch from
our farm to join the highway, starting the
work early in 1908. The road was started at
the river, the highway being graded and
leveled, with stumps and stones removed, and
gravel and sand were hauled from the river to
fill it in. Its entire construction occupied
the warm months during both 1908 and 1909, and
my father was not allowed any part of the
expense for labor or materials by the county.
But it was a good road, and my father felt it
was quite worthy of the automobile he planned
to buy, and that his efforts would be rewarded
by the pleasure we would derive from a car.

From right to left: John & Hattie, Myra, Clarence,
Leslie, Johnny, Helen, & Stanley.

# CHAPTER XII

The year, 1909, proved another eventful epoch in our lives.

By the time spring came the lumber company had hauled away the last of the logs above and below our farm. The logs on our farm, however, could not be touched by the lumber company without a settlement with my father, for he was at that time the legal owner of the logs.

Therefore, they came no nearer to our farm than the camp a mile away for, as I have said, no attempt to redeem the logs washed on our land at the time the dam went out was ever made. When the lumber company hauled away the last of their own logs, they made it clear that all hostilities with John Dietz were ended because the company had no further use for Cameron Dam. We felt, however, that as long as the great quantity of logs lay on our land, our farm was an object of interest to the lumber company. That remains for the reader to determine for himself!

Early in the spring my mother was ill for some time and when she was able to make the trip, she went to Rice Lake to see a doctor. He told her that she had been having attacks of appendicitis and would either have to undergo an operation or go on a rigid diet. My mother disliked the idea of an operation, and returning to our home she started on a diet so meager that one wonders how she ever survived. For fifty-six days she ate no solid food whatever, consuming only small portions of broth, a glass of hot milk or tea and other liquid foods. She warded off the appendicitis attacks and lost sixty pounds!

My father and the boys finished the road to the highway in the summer months, and we felt that the new automobile would be ours in the near future. The hunting season was unusually prosperous for many hunters brought their wives that year and we received a good revenue for meals and lodging. My father suffered a severe accident in September of that year when a delayed discharge of dynamite blew him about fifty feet. His arm was hurt and he suffered severe bruises when he came in contact with the hard ground. By the time the hunting season opened, however, he had improved sufficiently to act as guide and assistant to the many hunters we entertained.

The hunting crowd had thinned down to the Bangor Hunting Club and a few others by November 21. Early in the morning of that day my little brother Stanley, aged 8, came to my bed crying that he was sick. We immediately began treating him for a severe cold, but at six that evening he died of plural pneumonia. My brother, Leslie, became ill at the same time, and lay for weeks afterward at the point of death. Miss Myrtis Wallace, who was there with her uncle, Michigan Elliott, to get her deer, also became ill. The minister at Winter could not be obtained, for he was also ill at the time, and the members of the hunting club and Mr. Elliott gave little Stanley a Masonic funeral on that cold winter day, digging his grave and burying him on the "mountain peak" in a grove of trees. My Mother and I could not go to the grave, so ill were Leslie and Myrtis. Neither of them was able to be up and about until after the holidays. Myrtis had shot a deer, but the law will allow no deer removed after December 10th so we used it as part of the family food.

We had many visitors during the illness of Leslie and Myrtis, the most faithful of them being Father Beaudette, assistant to Dean Schmit of St. Joseph's Church at Rice Lake.

During the winter of 1909-1910 my father started negotiations with many parties concerning the sawing of the logs which lay on our farm. He finally signed a contract with the Howe Brothers Sawmill Company, of Faribault, Minnesota. This company agreed to bring in a sawmill and cut the logs into lumber suitable for a new house for one third of the logs. As soon as the roads were passable in the spring, the sawmill was moved in, and activities began. The work took all summer. A log scaler was present after the work was done and the lumber was evenly divided as agreed upon. Both piles of lumber, one belonging to us and the other to the sawmill company, were piled up on the field away from any danger of fire. We expected to start a new home the following spring, for we felt that we had long since outgrown our log cabin home, but fate again took a hand in our destiny. The lumber company hauled their logs out in September, for we had one of the most beautiful autumns Wisconsin had ever enjoyed.

*To our readers ... Thank you for helping get the word out!*

*Unlike writers who rely upon "brick and mortar" publishers, independent authors depend on our readers to spread the word about our books. If you're enjoying this annotated memoir, please let others know. Every purchase helps inspire more stories. Books make wonderful gifts. Copies ordered from BadgerValley.com are signed and shipped free to any USA address, including our servicemen and women. Again, thanks for your help.*

This Dietz family portrait was taken two weeks prior to Myra and her brothers being ambushed. Left to right are Myra, Helen, Hattie, John and Johnny, Leslie, and Clarence. The thumbprint on Leslie's jacket is probably that of the visiting reporter who developed the photo.

Posing for the newspapermen are (L to R) Deputies Roy Van Alstine and Fred Thorbahn, Sheriff Madden, and District Attorney J. C. Davis. Note that Van Alstine and Thorbahn each carry a pair of Luger pistols.

October 1, 1910, was the most important day of my life.

The day started out tamely enough—it was Saturday and we baked our usual twelve loaves of bread, with a half dozen pies and cakes thrown in for good measure at odd moments. In fact, it was after lunch before things began happening.

My father and the boys, Clarence, then 23, and Leslie, 19, were preparing to drive to town for our mail and the weekly supplies, when Floyd Gibbons, reporter for the *Chicago Tribune\**, arrived at the farm. He said he wanted to interview my father and get a real true story for the *Tribune* readers. My father was always courteous to newspaper reporters, so he turned to the boys and told them to go on and get the mail and supplies for he would stay at home with Mr. Gibbons. The boys suggested that I go with them, since Father couldn't go!

I had the queerest feeling about going with the boys—somehow I just didn't want to go! That seemed strange, for it was a beautiful day, warm and sunny, and I dearly loved the trip to the town through the woods and surely I enjoyed meeting my friends in the village. But the boys insisted that I go with them for the three of us could sing as we drove along and laugh and joke so the way seemed much shorter. I finally dressed in the new black brilliantine suit and the little white thin blouse which I had ordered from a mail order catalogue, and the three of us started to town about two o'clock.

*Actually, Gibbons wrote for the *Minneapolis Tribune* at the time.

We drove over the three miles of roadway built by my father and the boys, and out on the main highway. We had driven only a half mile on the main highway, and were trotting along at a good gait, all three of us singing at the tops of our lusty young voices, when suddenly a wild yell rang out and bullets began pouring into our surrey. I was sitting on the knees of my two brothers, for we had removed all but one of the surrey seats, and with the first fusillade of bullets I dropped into the bottom of the buggy at the boys' feet. Clarence was driving the team, a span of young horses he had himself broken to harness, and at the sound of the shooting they tried to run away.

Of course, Clarence's first thought was to hold the team to keep more damage from being done. Leslie, on the left, the side from which the bullets came, jumped over the lines and ran into the thick woods on the right side of the road. There, he dropped behind a log, and watched the enemies' next move. He had a Luger pistol with him, which he had carried with the intention of shooting partridges on the way home to have for Sunday dinner. It would have been an easy matter for him to shoot the men who appeared from the bushes, but he carefully considered the matter and did not take his gun from the holster.

As soon as the horses were halted, three men with their faces blackened like negroes, stepped from the thick underbrush at the left of the road with guns leveled upon us. One of the men—we afterwards learned he was Sheriff Madden—was trembling and frightened—"I didn't shoot! I didn't shoot!" he kept saying. He went to the horses' heads and held them by the

bits while the other two men came to the side
of the surrey and told us to hold up our
hands. I still lay in the bottom of the buggy,
scarcely conscious of what was happening, but
one of the men jerked me up by the arm and
told me to hold up my hands.

"Myra's shot!" said Clarence. But that fact
did not keep the men from starting to search
me for a gun.

"She hasn't a gun," said Clarence. "In that
thin little suit where would she have it?" The
men searched Clarence then, but he had no gun
either. I was jerked into the seat of the
buggy, and then I became fully conscious. I
looked up into the face of the man who was
putting handcuffs on me and recognized him
despite his blackened face.

"Why, you are Van Alstyne!" I said.

He told me to shut up and swore at me.

Clarence, too, was handcuffed, and placed
in the seat with me. Then Sheriff Madden
climbed into the buggy beside me and drove the
team, whipping the horses to a run, and the
two other men stood up in the back, holding to
the seat of the buggy. I had noticed a
stinging sensation in my side when they jerked
me from the bottom of the buggy, but now as
the horses raced over the rough road, I became
conscious of a terrible pain in my back. I
begged them to drive more slowly, but they
only laughed at me and said I wasn't shot,
that the bullet just grazed my side a little!
I knew I must be shot quite badly, for I
became so faint and weak, but I leaned against
my brother Clarence and tried to be brave.

When we crossed the Brunette River, two
miles from Winter, I asked the men to get me a
drink of water for I was so thirsty, but they

refused to stop. In this fashion we were taken into Winter.

We had one consolation, however! We knew that Leslie was safe! When he disappeared into the woods after his jump from the buggy, the men fired several shots after him, but they hesitated about going into the woods after him, evidently fearing he carried a gun and would use it. When he heard them discussing the question of coming into the woods after him, he started crawling through the underbrush, and after crawling for some distance he rose to his feet and ran toward home as fast as could go. At the top of the hill where our home-made road turned off the highway, he came out in the middle of the road and called to us. When we looked back he waved his arms in a signal to let us know he was all right. One of the men suggested unhitching one of the horses and riding back to look for him, but I had no fear that the boy would be caught in the woods—he was too good a woodsman for that!

When Leslie reached our farm he told my father and mother the news—stating he knew I had been shot from the way I dropped from their knees to the bottom of the buggy. My father's first thought was for us and wanted to go to Winter at once. Mr. Gibbons, the *Tribune* reporter, was still there, and he joined with my mother in urging my father not to go, for he would only rake more trouble for himself and would probably not be allowed to see us anyway. Mr. Gibbons volunteered to go into the village and get news of us and return to the farm. I don't know how he got into the village of Winter, but my mother tells how he came riding back a few hours later on an

Indian pony, bareheaded, to bring my parents the news that I was alive but badly wounded, and that Clarence was in jail.

When Sheriff Madden and his deputies reached Winter with us, they stopped at the village hotel long enough to carry me into the little ladies' parlor and then took Clarence over to the village jail. They had no warrant of any kind for his arrest, but he was held in that jail for a few hours and then taken to the county jail at Hayward in an automobile where he was held for a week.

In the little hotel parlor, Mrs. Phelan took off my clothes and put a nightdress on me. With the removal of my old fashioned steel-ribbed corset—that was the day when such instruments of torture were considered indispensible for the well-dressed girl—the blood began to pour from the wounds in my side and back. Dr. Burns, who had just located in the village, was called. He looked at my wounds and put on some anti-septic powder and some bandages. For a while they left me lying on the lumpy little sofa in the parlor, but before night I was taken upstairs and placed in a bedroom. Mrs. Phelan and a school teacher, Miss Deuster, sat with me by turns and gave me bits of ice to melt in my parched mouth. After the doctor's casual bandaging of my wounds that Saturday afternoon he never re-appeared. The county coroner at Hayward was called, and he arrived about dusk. He was a physician, but he never examined my wounds, he just looked at me and left some pills which I later learned were morphine, and departed. The pills were administered at fairly regular intervals, and these, with the ice bits, were all the treatment I had until midnight Monday night. No food passed my mouth.

After the coroner had visited me, a deputy sheriff and the town marshal were stationed outside my door. The town was placed under martial law, for feelings ran high when the report that three innocent children had been shot down in cold blood. Telegraph wires were out so that no messages could come in or go out and the highways were guarded.

Despite all these precautions, Floyd Gibbons, the intrepid reporter, came into my room to talk to me. He told me that he had been out to the farm and that Leslie was all right, and my father was being urged to remain at home to save his own life. He said I should not be afraid for he would be right with me, looking after me, until they took me to a hospital. His reassurances were most comforting. Remember that I was just a country kid—and my thrilling experience of that Saturday afternoon, coupled with the intense pain and the fear of what would happen next, would have been bad enough in familiar surroundings but there I was for the first time in my life alone in a hotel room, with my door guarded by armed men. I had done no wrong to anyone—I was merely the daughter of a man who had defended his rights. My brother was in jail because he was a son of the same man—what would happen to him? And my parents and small brothers and sister on the farm—what was being plotted against them? It all seemed a terrible nightmare!

Mr. Gibbon's friendly declaration of sympathy was most gratefully received. I knew he would do just what he said, and the sound of his typewriter in the next room as he

tapped out his story of our misfortunes later
that evening was a friendly little tune! As he
sat beside my bed I told him that I recognized
Roy Van Alstyne, one of the men who shot me
even though his face and hands were blackened
and his clothes those of a lumberman. Van
Alstyne, I told him, was one of our neighbors,
a man with a good wife and two small children
which he treated shamefully. Our family felt
sorry for them, and frequently gave them milk
and eggs when their supplies were low. Many
times, too, we brought the wife and little
ones over to stay with us for several days at
a time while Mr. Van Alstyne was away on one
of his drunken debauches. He, too, often
called at the house and would sit beside the
stove talking to my father and the boys for
hours at a time. We did not know Sheriff
Madden, for he had been elected that spring,
and we had never seen him. The third man, we
later learned, was Fred Thorbin, who had
drifted into the village of Winter shortly
before. It was learned then that he had been
in serious difficulties in the Dakotas, his
wife having died under circumstances that
pointed to Mr. Thorbin's guilt, although he
was able to get himself freed.

Thorbin and Van Alstyne had been deputized
by Sheriff Madden, Mr. Gibbons told me, and it
was one of the two who shot me. Thorbin later
bragged that it was he whose gun brought me
down, and that he received $20,000 from some
source for his act!

Mr. Gibbons typed out his story in the next
room, after he had talked to me, but when he
went to the telegraph office to send it to his
paper, he found the wires cut. But that didn't
stop him. Although he had spent a busy day, he

took his story and hiked down the railroad to Radisson, six miles away, where he was able to put his story on the wire. There was no sleep for Mr. Gibbons that night.*

All day Sunday I lay in a sort of stupor. I was weak and sick, but I didn't feel much pain, due to the morphine that was given me constantly. Mrs. Phelan, the landlord's wife, was most kind to me, but she told me that I mustn't tell it, because she and her husband were "afraid" to express their sympathy for me and my family. I don't know whom they feared. Floyd Gibbons was in and out all day. On one of his visits he told of visiting the spot where the shots had been fired at my brothers and me. He said he found the bushes and logs behind which the Sheriff and his "deputies" had lain concealed—and there he discovered a neat little stack of empty whiskey bottles, mute evidence that the "officers of the law" had been well liquored up for the performance of their dangerous duty. It takes nerve, indeed, to shoot down three young folks singing down the road.

I saw no members of my family during the time I was at the hotel, for they refused to allow Clarence to see me before taking him to jail at Hayward. Mr. Gibbons, however, promised to deliver my messages to my parents

*Other reports say Floyd Gibbons filed his news item via telephone from Winter, then cut the wires to assure he'd have an exclusive feature story, nationwide. Days later he was arrested for this and spent a week in jail, missing the siege on the farm the following week. Gibbons was fired by the *Minneapolis Daily Tribune* but later hired by the *Chicago Tribune* where he became famous for his on-site coverage of WWI and later reporting.

as soon as he could get through the lines of "deputies" who guarded every road.

Many people tried to get into town or to our farm to help us, but even at Ladysmith, Draper and Radisson, towns six to twenty-eight miles away, everyone who got off the trains was questioned and warned to stay away from Winter. A party of twenty men, headed by Doctor Kleinschmidt, of Milwaukee, came to Ladysmith with the intention of driving direct to the farm to aid my father, but when they got off the train they found they would have to start fighting their way through at once. They became discouraged and turned around and went back. My uncle, W. W. Dietz, tried to get in with a party of men, but was also turned back. The shooting affair was well planned, and thoroughly carried out!

At seven o'clock, on Monday, October 3, two armed deputies and Mrs. Phelan came into my room and after wrapping me in blankets they put me on a stretcher with my face covered with a sheet. I was carried through the street about three blocks to the railroad station and placed in the center of a freight car, with the ends of the car filled with trunks and big freight boxes. I was familiar with the train—I knew it was the combination freight and passenger train which ran to Rice Lake, sixty miles away. When my face was uncovered I saw the two deputies who had carried the stretcher, and three others whom I did not know sitting on kitchen chairs in the car, evidently prepared to take the trip with me. Mrs. Deuster, mother of the school teacher, was also with us.

The train started with the usual jerk of a short line freight train, and we were on our way—but what our destination would be I had not the slightest idea! The train stopped at Radisson and Mrs. Deuster got off, leaving me alone in the freight car with the five men. There were no windows in the car, and no ventilation, but the men sat in their kitchen chairs and smoked their pipes and talked. The train stopped at each station along the way, and the big doors would be thrown open as the express men hauled their wagons up to the car, great freight boxes and trunks would be dumped with loud crashes on the floor of the freight car. How it hurt me!

As we passed through Hayward, a new supply of morphine pills and a cake of ice were taken aboard, and the pills and bits of cracked ice were given to me frequently along the way.

In the middle of the afternoon, I noticed an unusual activity among the men in the car. They frequently opened the doors of the freight car—the only way they could see outside—and peered about. I forced my wandering mind to listen to what they were saying and I heard them speak of my uncle.

"That W. W. Dietz may be here!" I heard one man say. "He is as bad as John Dietz, and is a good shot, too." "If they do come," said another of the men, "at the first false move, start shooting, and shoot to kill!"

I was glad, indeed, that I might see my uncle, but was mortally afraid that another shooting affair would be started and didn't feel that my nerves could stand another. But my uncle was too smart to start anything of that kind. He had been a sheriff many years and he knew that officers would resist any efforts to take their prisoner away, even though she was an innocent person, desperately

wounded through their bungling efforts at
"justice." He came into the car where I was
and talked to me. He got down on his knees and
put his arms about me and kissed me. The tears
streamed down his cheeks when I told him I
didn't know where I was shot, but it must be
somewhere through my body for I couldn't move,
and my side and back hurt terribly. He stayed
with me while the freight car I was in was
switched to another train and then he was
forced to leave me while I resumed my journey
with the same five men. The train to which the
car was then attached to the main line and was
faster than the first one. The track was no
smoother, however, and the car bounced and
jerked and lurched just as much as ever.

At ten o'clock that night we arrived at
Ashland. The hospital ambulance met the train
and the stretcher and I were loaded into it
and taken direct to the hospital. Dr. J. M.
Dodd, head physician of St. Joseph's hospital,
Sister Josephine, surgical nurse, and other
nurses were apparently waiting for me, for I
was rushed into the operating room after a
short examination.

When the bandages were removed, I heard Dr.
Dodd say to the sisters: "The traitors! This
girl has had no medical attention—just some
little antiseptic gauzes!" Then for the first
time I learned how badly I had been shot.
According to Dr. Dodd's report the bullet
entered my body at the left side at the waist
line, just over the hip bone, passing through
the left kidney and lower bowels and through
the spinal region, coming out one quarter of
an inch to the right of the spine, shattering
the vertebra. The doctor and his nurses found
that a steel jacketed bullet had been used in

the shooting, and it had passed right through me. Clarence had suffered a slight flesh wound on the arm just above the elbow at the time I was shot and it was believed that the bullet which passed through me had gone on and grazed his arm.

My wounds were cleansed and I was put to bed in a spotless white room, with a bell at my bedside so I could ring if I wanted anything. Everyone was kind to me, but I was positively scared to death! I had never seen a hospital before, and the sights and the odors and the operating room made me think that I was just being brought in there to be murdered. It was the first time I had ever seen a Catholic sister, and the long gowns and the big white and black headgear added to my fright. In the weeks that followed I surely had a change of heart for their kindness and gentleness were as healing as their medicines.

Soon I was put to bed, blood began to pour from my mouth and I rang the bell frantically to call the sister. She came in and said: "Don't be alarmed, we had expected that!" As my wound had bled very little on the outside, the blood had just filled my body until I was swollen three times my normal size. Then the long bumpy ride caused a hemorrhage. The flow of blood continued all night, but the sisters were kindness itself to me.

Their efforts to take care of me were slightly hampered by the presence of Deputy Sheriff Arentson, one of the men who had accompanied me from Winter. He insisted on sitting right in the room to "guard" me. How the hospital authorities hated him and his arrogance! The Sisters complained that it wasn't right for a man to be in a girl's room that way, prisoner or no prisoner! But it was several days before sufficient pressure could be brought to bear upon him to get him out of the room. Then he was removed to the hall, where he occupied a chair just outside my door. No warrant had been issued for my arrest—there was no reason why a deputy sheriff should be guarding me like a hardened criminal, but there he was, and there he remained! He opened all my mail, and what he wanted me to have was permitted to be passed on—the rest was confiscated.

I was permitted to see no visitors for a week—the nurses prohibiting them because of my condition, and the deputy sheriff prohibiting them on general principles, I guess. But one visitor scorned hospital rules and officers alike and walked into my room. That visitor was Burt Williams, editor of the *Ashland Press*, at that time, and now holding a state office and living at Milwaukee. Mr. Williams said he was a friend of our family and that I should ask him for anything I wanted. I told him I wanted news of my family most of all. After that he wired and kept posted on all the news concerning our family and he was able to tell me where Clarence had been taken and what was going on in Winter and Sawyer County.

Then one day he came in and told me the most distressing news I had yet heard. A posse was being formed in Sawyer County to go to the farm and take my father, mother, my brothers and my sister, dead or alive!

## DIETZ FIGHT OVER

### Says Dietz Will Build Mill and Cut up Logs.

LADYSMITH, Wis., June 16.—W. W. Dietz of Rice Lake, brother of John Dietz, thinks the fight at Cameron dam is over. The logging companies have spent more than $100,000 trying to move a quarter million dollars' worth of logs from the Cameron dam pond and the last of a half dozen squads of deputies sent there has left with the statement that nothing but a criminal warrant will do the business. The logging company at first involved tried to get a criminal warrant and, failing, transferred their claim to the logs to an interstate concern in order to get into the United States courts, but here again a criminal warrant was refused. Feeling that at one time was very favorable to the logging concerns has turned into sympathy for Dietz.

It is now now reported that Dietz purposes putting in a sawmill and cutting up enough of the 20,000,000 feet of pine now held to cover his claims against the logging companies. —Milwaukee Journal.

## FLED LIKE COWARDS

### Wounded Man Tells How He Was Left To Die By His Companions.

Radisson, Wis., July 31.—After crawling on his hands and knees for a distance through the forest, Duyo Rogich, of Milwaukee, wounded in three places by Clarence Dietz, reached the homestead of Charles Johnson and was later carried into Winter, where he secured medical attention. Slight hope is entertained for his recovery. He had been terribly exposed when he reached the Johnson place his wounds had become filled with dirt.

Rogich told the story of his terrible experience to the conductor of the Hayward train.

### LADYSMITH NEWS-BUDGET

# WAR ON CHILDREN

### SHERIFF MADDEN HIDES IN AMBUSH AND DISTINGUISHES HIMSELF.

## DIETZ COMING TO TOWN

### Defender of Cameron Dam Laughs at Terrible Village's Plans.—Small Army Defends Town Against the Desperate Man.

Winter. — Two children of John Deitz are under arrest, the boy Clarence, with a slight wound in his arm, and the daughter, Myra, in a critical condition, with a bullet thru her abdomen.

Sheriff Madden decided Saturday evening to make an effort to stop public criticism of his failure to get Deitz, and posted an ambuscade along the road to Winter, expecting Deitz to come for his mail. Instead of Deitz, three of his children, unarmed were the victims, and when they laughed at Madden's commands to hold up their hands, the sheriff and his posse opened fire at fifteen feet and after a rain of bullets the girl and one boy fell, while the younger boy escaped through the woods to their house.

# Chapter XIV

The worry and anxiety at our farm home over my condition must have been intense, from the story my mother tells of those days. They saw no one from that Saturday when we were shot to the following Wednesday. Then two men appeared across the river and crossed to our farm over the footbridge. When they reached the house they told my father they were representing Governor Davidson, and had come to take my father out with them.

My father was delighted that Governor Davidson had at last shown a disposition to help our cause by protecting him and his family, and invited the men to come into the house to talk things over. One of the men introduced himself as Colonel Munson, private secretary to Governor Davidson, and the other as Mr. Gilbert, also a member of the Governor's staff. My father naturally asked to see their credentials, but they informed him they carried nothing whatever to identify themselves.

"I would, like to go with you, if you are from the governor," said my father. "But my children have been shot down in cold blood and taken away from home. When officers stoop low enough to do that, I don't know what their next move will be. How can I trust you and go out myself, or take my family with me, when you have nothing to show us your good intentions!"

The men agreed with him that it would be an unwise thing, and departed, telling him they would go to Winter and wire the governor for the proper credentials. Instead of doing that they went out and reported that my father had refused to accompany them and therefore deserved no sympathy.

Immediately a posse of twenty lumberjacks and thrill-loving young men of Winter, led by Thorbin and Van Alstyne, were sworn in and plans were made to capture my family—dead or alive!

My father and mother had no means of knowing the posse was being formed, but great fear for the safety of the family was constantly felt that week. A look-out was maintained each night, and the children were kept well dressed for a hasty removal was expected every moment. They discussed the possibility of slipping away in the night—but where could they go? There was only one road, and they knew it was guarded for neither my uncle nor anyone else had been able to get out to the farm that week! My mother and the little children couldn't walk through the woods! And even if they did get through, how would they be treated in the village of Winter, where the rest of us had been so unfortunate. It was a bitter week for the family—but the final battle came on Saturday, just a week from the day I was shot.

Of course I was not there—I was lying in the hospital at Ashland, but my mother tells the story as I repeat it here.

My brother Leslie and sister, Helen, then 9 years of age, went out in the field early Saturday morning to drive the cows in to be milked. When they were close to the "mountain peak", near Stanley's grave, a volley of bullets were fired at them, one bullet passing through Leslie's trousers leg near the calf of his leg. The cows were excited and jumped to their feet and began to run, and the frightened children ran back to the house. My father had heard the shooting and ran to meet the children—then all of them went into the house. That seemed to be the signal for general firing from every direction.

The clearing on which the house and barn stood was entirely surrounded by armed men, who poured hundreds of shots into the home. My mother took the little ones into the kitchen where the walls were thickest and put them behind the cook stove while the bullets popped about over the floor.

The log walls stopped many bullets, but others would pass through the chinks or the windows. The glass was shattered on the enlarged picture of the family which hung on the  living room wall; other bullets passed through the back of my mother's rocking chair; in fact, scarcely a piece of furniture remained undamaged. Not a man was in sight around the farm—the bullets came from the woods on all sides, but not a person came into view. My father stood with his gun ready to shoot anyone who appeared, but he hadn't a chance to fire a single shot.

At last the firing became so bad that my father said he would go to the barn and perhaps draw the fire there and save the lives of my mother and the children. He took his hat, coat and gun, and walked rapidly to the barn. Not a single shot was fired at him as he made the trip. And, once he was inside the barn, the firing at the home continued as strong as before, with an additional bombardment of the barn. At last, he thought of the little window at the rear, the window where someone had climbed in the year before to stab one of our horses, and he opened it to look out. As he put his hand up to the latch, a bullet hit the palm of his hand.

Suffering from the severe pain, he ran back to the house with the bullets peppering his pathway. My mother and the children had miraculously escaped injury, but our little brown spaniel lay dying in the yard with a bullet through his body. The bullets were still pouring into the home, and my mother and father decided that some desperate action must be taken. But what should it be? My mother argued that surely we must have friends out there—surely my father's brother had come or there was someone who would help us if a white flag were waved. But who should wave it? If either my father or mother appeared they would be shot down instantly—and my mother said: "Let Helen go!" No sooner were the words out of her mouth than little Helen seized the towel and ran into the yard, waving it above her head. Instantly the firing ceased!

Later, we learned that Father Pilon had been with the posse of men, imploring them to cease firing, and all his begging and pleading availing nothing. But when the white flag appeared, he ordered; "Cease firing!" with authority. He then ran forward and caught Helen up in his arms. The posse also came in from every direction and entered the house. They seized my father, and said: "You killed a man! You killed Harp when you shot him from the barn!"

They swore at him and tried to put handcuffs on him, but my father said he was not the kind of man who needed handcuffs, and they didn't put any on him.

The firing had continued until sometime in the afternoon—my mother could never remember the hour when it stopped. She was given a few minutes to pick up a few clothes for the children. In addition to those she took her precious tin box with the family records and the money which she had dug up from its hiding place the day after I was shot. The men tried to take the tin box away from her, but by that time sufficient friends had reached the house to stop the theft. My father and Leslie were taken in one car and my mother and the children rode in another car with the driver, Father Pilon and a reporter. All were taken to Hayward, where my father was placed in a cell in the county jail.

John and Leslie Dietz
Sawyer County Jail, Hayward, Wis

My mother, Leslie and the children were kept in the home of the sheriff, which is under the roof of the jail, until, it was decided what disposition should be made of them. When the posse entered our home, they were led by Sheriff Madden, Thorbin and Van Alstyne, the three men who had shot me just a week before. My father risked another shooting by telling them what he thought of men who would lie in ambush and fire on innocent children—but my father was noted for speaking his mind.

No reason was given then for the shooting of myself and my brothers, and to this day, none has been given! When the men came to the buggy that day when I lay wounded, Clarence said: "We have done nothing. Why are you shooting us?"

The men swore at him and answered: "You are just as bad as your father!"

Sheriff Madden, Thorbin and Van Alstyne tried to excuse our shooting on the grounds that they thought my father was with us, but that was disproved.

It was easy to see, however, how our shooting led to the raid on the home. Public sentiment ran so high and so much feeling was aroused by the shooting of the innocent members of the family that the officers felt they should do something immediately to turn the tide in their favor. They wanted to make it appear that it was necessary for the sheriff and two deputies to lie in wait along the roadside and pick off John Dietz before he got a shot at them. That it was only the children going to town was merely an unfortunate occurrence over which the officers had no control, they tried to reason to the public. They wanted to make it plain that John Dietz had always remained in his farm strong hold, armed to the teeth, and ready to pick off any officer who appeared with a warrant for his arrest. If they wanted John Dietz at any time during the four years since Clarence had been shot, he could easily have been taken. If the officers didn't want to come to the farm for him why didn't they arrest him on one of his weekly trips to Winter for supplies—or when he went down to Rice Lake on visits? In the four years following the shooting of Clarence, none of my family ever saw an officer unless it was a casual meeting on the village streets. None came to our home and no papers of any kind were ever served upon my father. Why were we children shot—and why did the posse keep firing into the home where my mother and my little brothers and sister were when they knew my father was in the barn?

These are questions we asked then, and are still asking. There has never been a reply to them.

And all those "warrants" and "indictments" which the officers and the grand jury had been talking about for six years! We would like to know what became of them. They were never mentioned after my father was lodged in the county jail at Hayward.

The charge placed against him at that time was that he climbed to the haymow during the time he was in the barn on the day of the raid, and from that point had fired upon and killed one Oscar Harp, who was creeping on his hands and knees from the woods to the piles of lumber which lay at some distance from the house.

My father did not do it.

He did not climb to the haymow while in the barn—it would have been a foolish thing to do for the thin roof of the barn was literally peppered with bullets. Then, too, the haymow was only half full of hay and would have offered no opportunity for a man to climb up and peer out of the top of the roof.

Despite these facts, my father was accused of the murder and held in jail without bail.

Immediately after the shooting up of our home, Clarence was released from the county jail at Hayward, where he had been held to keep him away from the farm during the raid. He was allowed to go free, but the officers tried to get warrants for my mother and Leslie, saying they had "shot at" the posse. But Father Pilon and others who had been present knew that the Dietz family had no opportunity to shoot and no charge could be obtained. After a week at the sheriff's quarters, my mother, brothers and sister, Helen, went to the home of my married sister, May, at Cameron Junction, Wisconsin.

Elmyra Dietz - Deputy Sheriff Carson
Ashland, Wis., Oct 21st 1910

When the news was brought to me that our home had been raided, my mother and the children driven out, and my father lodged in jail, I was conscious of a great relief that none had been killed. It seemed almost incredible that so much shooting had taken place with no lives lost. My thoughts turned then to getting well so I could work to get my father out of jail.

I had been under close observation ever since my arrival, and at last, two weeks after I arrived at the hospital, I was again removed to the operating room and operated upon. I was desperately frightened at the thought of the operation but Dr. Dodd's little blonde secretary, Miss Petersen, came to my room that morning and talked to me for a long while and helped get me ready. Then she went to the operating room and held my hand until I was given the anesthetic. Two incisions had to be made, one where the bullet entered the side, and another where it came out at the back. At the side a drainage tube was put into the kidney to remove the pus, and each day until the week before Christmas that tube had to be removed and the wound probed. I was such a healthy young person that the wound would heal over on the outside before the inside was properly drained if the tube had been allowed to remain untouched, as in most operations. At the incision in the back, two pieces of vertebra about the size of the doctor's thumbnail were removed.

A few days after my operation, the hospital authorities found that my birthday would be October 30th, and the story that Myra Dietz would celebrate her twenty-second birthday in the hospital was published in the newspapers. What a flood of letters and birthday cards I received—they came pouring in from every state in the union. And the lovely gifts! I shall remember them always. Beautiful handkerchiefs and scarfs came in every mail. And I received more than three hundred dollars in money. Some of it came in envelopes in one, two or five dollar bills suggesting that I buy myself a birthday present. Mayor Keller, of St. Paul, sent me fifty dollars, and a Stenographers' Club of Minneapolis, headed by Miss Thurston, sent me one hundred dollars. The money was surely appreciated, too. The time was coming when I would need clothes, for I had come into the hospital in nothing but a borrowed nightdress!

My room was kept banked with beautiful flowers all the time I was in the hospital, chiefly furnished by the Men's City Club, of Ashland, and an ice cream company sent me a pint of ice cream every day I lay in the hospital. And kind people sent in fruit enough to supply not only myself but all the wards in the hospital. The sisters brought a little tinkling music box into my room. In fact, everything that could possibly be done to make my stay pleasant was tried.

I had many visitors—some came to see me because I was sick and alone—others just to look at me, I suppose, out of curiosity. The first Sunday I was in the hospital, I was propped up in bed and the door was opened so the steady stream of visitors who walked through the corridor could look in at me. I rather enjoyed them—I had seen so few strange faces in my life! And little children left a heap of little gifts at my door!

The deputy, Arentson, was finally removed from the hospital after he had been chased from my room to the hall and from the hall to the front door. Put out by easy stages, one might say.

When I was able to be placed in a wheel chair, Sister Josephine would wheel me to the elevator and then to chapel each Sunday morning. Both Mr. Williams and Dr. Dodd took me to their homes for dinner. I was taken downtown by Mrs. DeCoursey, who furnished me a coat and dress for the trip, and there we bought a brand new outfit of clothes for me with my birthday money.

I had several theatrical offers while in the hospital. One of them for a western vaudeville tour at $1000 a week for ten weeks. The strangest offer I had was from a beauty and barber shop owner in Milwaukee who offered me $100 a week for a year to sit inside the barber shop and count the money! I was forced to reject all offers—I was not able to travel, badly as we needed the money. One leg was two inches shorter than the other, and I was weak and nervous when I was at last able to leave the hospital.

Sawyer County paid the doctor bill and my hospital expenses for the twelve weeks I had been at Ashland, and a few days before Christmas I was considered able to leave. I went to Rice Lake, to my grandparents where my mother was staying at that time.

It was not a happy Christmas that year. My father was in jail, held without bond—some of the children were at my sister's farm home, and the rest of us were staying with my

grandparents. Not much like the old happy
Christmases when a jovial Santa Claus asked if
we had all been good boys and girls!

A Dietz Defense Committee had been formed
in Milwaukee, soliciting funds for my father's
legal defense. Soon after Christmas I went to
Milwaukee and sat in the office of the Defense
Committee for a few hours each day. When my
brother Clarence and I arrived in Milwaukee
that day we were met at the train by the Mayor
of Milwaukee, the District Attorney and a
group of other prominent citizens who escorted
us to the offices of the Defense Committee in
the Gawker Building.

Our first "public appearance" was in the
Auditorium. Admission was free for the meeting
was to be something of a "mass meeting". How
the people flocked to see us. The great hall
of the Auditorium was packed to the rafters
doors before the meeting was scheduled to
open, and several thousands were turned away.
I was helped to the stage, for my crippled
condition made walking difficult, and made a
little talk after a series of speeches by the
mayor and other prominent citizens.

I told where I had been shot and pointed to
my side and my back, and related the
circumstances of the shooting—the men with
blackened faces hiding in the bushes to shoot
us as we went singing along the road to town.
I thanked everyone for the expressions of
sympathy that had come to me in the hospital,
and told how splendidly I had been treated in
the hospital.

It was my first "speech", but I was not
troubled with stage fright. For six years we
had been talking to the highest and lowest in
the land—being interviewed by reporters,

writing our own stories for the newspapers and
having hundreds of columns written about us.
The only trouble I experienced was riding in
the sleeping car. I had never seen a berth on
the train, and I spent the night on that trip
from Rice Lake to Milwaukee in No. 10, but I
certainly didn't take off my clothes. I didn't
sleep, either! I had survived a flood and a
shooting but those queer little beds shut off
with such inadequate green curtains frightened
me far worse. It seemed that some people spent
the entire night walking up and down the aisle
of the train, and I'm afraid my pale face when
we arrived in Milwaukee was not wholly due to
hospital pallor.

In Milwaukee I knew that newspaper
reporters were all set to talk about the kick
I would get out of the high buildings and
other city sights, for it was the first time I
had ever been in a big city. But I resolved
not to "gawk" at a thing, no matter how much I
wanted to look. So when someone would point
out one of the cherished city sights, I would
give it a bored glance as much as to say,
"Haven't you a really big building you can
show me?" But out of the corner of my eye I
would give it a good, sharp look and fix its
location in my memory so that someday I could
go back and give that building or monument or
park the best "looking-over" it ever had! I
had a great horror of appearing "countrified",
and I'm afraid that my unnatural reserve gave
many people a totally wrong impression.
Perhaps that helped people to believe I had
the iron nerve that many newspaper men had
reported.

At that "mass meeting" in the Auditorium, a
money box stood beside the door, into which

contributions to aid my father might be dropped. Over two thousand dollars were collected in that way. The Defense Committee had been going about the factories, before our arrival, making speeches and collecting money, so that the total amount of the contributions were tremendous. The Dietz family received not one cent of these contributions. The money was used by the lawyers in defraying travelling expenses to look up evidence, and in obtaining depositions, and in various other ways. Mismanagement was always suspected, but we were country folks, unused to the ways of the world, and most reluctant to make any suggestions that would give the impression we were not grateful for all that was done for us.

We wanted Clarence Darrow for our lawyer, but at the last moment, almost, he wired that he had taken the case of Will Haywood, the famous Socialist, and could not defend my father. The lawyer by the Minneapolis Defense Committee, Phillip Westfall, did a great deal of splendid work for us, but he could not take charge of my Father's trial because he belonged in a different state.

We began making plans for my father's defense at New Year's. But first, we wanted him out of jail on bail. The Milwaukee lawyers arranged matters so he could be let out if we raised the bail money. I was in Milwaukee then and I remembered our good friends, the Bangor Hunting Club, who had been at the farm when Stanley died. Accordingly, I got on the train for Bangor, crippled, weak and ill, and made the trip to Bangor. The club members met at the Elson home and in one evening arranged to put up $40,000 for the bonding company. That was the amount of bail required for my father's freedom.

I returned to Rice Lake to be there with my mother when my father was released. Leslie went to Hayward and brought my father back with him, and the family had its first reunion since that October day when I had been shot.

But we couldn't waste time on merry-making. My father's trial was set for the spring term of court, approximately the latter part of April, and already January was rapidly going.

Leslie and I were invited over to Minneapolis, where the Defense Committee of that city was working. We went over a few days before a meeting scheduled at the Shubert Theatre, and helped arrange the publicity. The use of the theatre was contributed at cost for the meeting, the offering being made by the Messrs. Shubert through Manager Bainbridge. We found the plans for the meeting were so elaborate that we wired my father, who was resting at Rice Lake, to come over and make his own speech.

The report of the meeting can best be told in the words of the reporter for the *Minneapolis Tribune*, who covered the meeting:

"It was John Dietz, the orator, who told the thrilling story of his fight with the 'lumber trust' to an audience that packed the Shubert Theatre last night. Earnest, self-composed, convincing in the narration of his troubles, Mr. Dietz seemed never to lack even for a moment, the right word to express himself. His constant use of pithy epigrams never failed to bring applause, and his repartee in answering questions after his main talk would have done credit to make a public speaker of repute.

"That the audience was with Mr. Dietz strongly was indicated on his introduction. His address was interrupted throughout with such cries as 'You're all right, John!' and apparently every man, woman, and child in the house stood as a testimonial of sympathy for his cause at the close.

"The curtain arose on a flag-draped stage with the orchestra playing patriotic airs. Beside the shot-riddled family organ, brought all the way from Cameron Dam last fall, sat Myra and Leslie Dietz. Inconspicuous among sympathizers for his cause sat the man whose experiences, possessing color of the dime novel hue, have startled readers of the entire country. He sat quietly, a big, kind looking man one leg crossed over the other, his eyes lifted to where the galleries were dotted with the faces of people bursting with enthusiasm.

"When, upon his introduction by Rev. G. L. Morrill, the applause had died out, John Dietz hastened to explain that he was not a speaker, that he had lived on a farm almost continuously since early boyhood and had never been trained in the arts of the platform.

"'Providence,' he began, 'has permitted me to meet the good people of Minneapolis and explain my side of the corporation conspiracy that has sought to deprive myself and people of life, liberty and happiness and it pleases me to be here. It is hard to tell what is lawful and what is unlawful, and when God's laws and man's laws conflict, I have chosen first for God's. I couldn't tell you all of my case inside of thirty years. The Lumber trust, by its own admission, has spent three million dollars to 'get Dietz'.'

"Then he launched into the detailed history of his difficulty with the lumber company, beginning with what he termed the Hayward election riot in 1902, and how, with the lumber corporation's knowing the feeling toward him in Hayward, he put up the notice on the dam in 1904 forbidding trespass.

"'They sought to crush me then,' he shouted, 'but they have failed.'

"Telling of his experience with the foreman of the lumber company when pay had been denied for work as watchman on Price Dam, Mr. Dietz explained that the foreman had called him a liar. 'I told him to guard his tongue,' said the speaker. 'He kept on abusing me and finally one of his men started at me from behind while the foreman came at me with his fists. I suppose I should have run, but wasn't made to run. If I had been made that way it would have saved much trouble. What I did was give the foreman an uppercut with my right and put him over the top of the bunk. Then I put his assistant to sleep.'

"It was during the recital of his fistic encounters and his verbal argument with state officials that the speaker received heartiest applause.

"'Our papers of title are admitted by the most expert attorneys to be without flaw,' said Mr. Dietz, in speaking of his property rights. 'It is untrue that I defended the dam with a shotgun. Is anyone so simple as to believe that one man with a shotgun can hold up the lumber trust? The lumber company exhausted every nefarious resource to get the upper hand. It even resorted to poisoning our dumb animals.'

"The Cameron Dam defender then went into detail of the many attempts at settlement that had been made, explaining the reasons for his attitude in each instance.

"'I always insisted,' he said, 'that all I wanted was rights between man and man. They thought I didn't know enough to come in out of the rain. They picked me for a fool and burnt their fingers. Some have told me that they supposed I was a big green Dutchman. After the first gun battle, I told my wife that the biggest battle we will have to contend with will be a battle of words. I beat my enemy with words and they resorted to brute force.'

"When Mr. Dietz had finished the recital of his case, he asked for questions from the audience and was furnished with a volley of them, which he answered quickly and often in humorous fashion.

"'Do you want to go back to Cameron Dam?' someone asked.

"'The family is inclined to go anywhere but there,' he answered. 'Since we have left the band of assassins up there, they are robbing one another.'

"'Did you do any shooting on the day you surrendered?' was asked.

"'No,' he answered. 'I looked all day for an opportunity.'

"In concluding he said, 'I have been asked if I am a Socialist. I am no kind of an 'ist', but I do believe we need a housecleaning in Sawyer County.'

"Myra Dietz was also one of the speakers last night, referring to her experiences in being shot, to which there were many cries of 'Oh!' and 'The cowards!' Leslie Dietz assisted in explaining the pictures of Cameron dam which were thrown on a screen, and little Clarence Booth sang a solo.

At that meeting, we charged admission and took in $1,800. The meeting was repeated the following Friday night, and we cleared $800 after paying $400 for the use of the theatre. We were in Minneapolis several weeks, during which meetings were held in various halls and churches where contributions were taken.

Many interesting occurrences took place, the one copied from the *Tribune* here being particularly thrilling:

"Laughter and tears were mingled, at the Unique theatre yesterday morning during the progress of the People's Church service, conducted by Rev. G, L. Morrill, a major portion of the service being a benefit for the John Dietz defense fund.

"Almyra and Leslie Dietz occupied seats in one of the boxes. Both were introduced to the audience which completely filled the theatre, and Leslie addressed the gathering very briefly. Hundreds crowded about the main entrance unable to gain admittance, the entire stage space was packed solid and many uncomplainingly remained standing throughout the entire service.

"In the midst of the collection, taken towards the close of the service, an aged woman waveringly tottered to the center of the footlights and handed Revs Mr. Morrill a 5-cent piece, explaining in a whisper that it was all the money she had. With tears streaming down her face she turned and worked her way to the rear amid great applause. Many in the audience wept with her. Apparently she paid no heed and kept her identity to herself, although the offering was doubtless her car fare home. Rev. Mr. Morrill immediately offered the coin to the highest bidder and it was ultimately knocked down to a woman spectator who paid $10 for it."

Two beautiful flags were presented to us in Minneapolis to take the place of the flag which had been shot from the flagpole beside our home at Cameron Dam on the day of the raid. We visited many other Minnesota towns while on that trip and by that time my father had found a comfortable home where the whole family could room and board together. The home was in Rice Lake where we had lived during our early years.

Soon after we were settled, another boy was born to my mother. That was the tenth child in our family. My mother had been under so great a strain, however, during the past few months that the poor little chap didn't have a chance to begin life a healthy normal baby. He died within a few days, and was buried at Rice Lake. My mother did not recover her health for many months.

My father and I made a trip into the southern part of Wisconsin, making public appearances and speaking at various gatherings to keep the sentiment of the people in our favor before the trial began. My brothers, Leslie and Clarence, went to Duluth and surrounding towns on the same errand. Then we all met at Rice Lake and accompanied father to Hayward for the trial in the latter part of April.

# LIBERTY FOR BOY

## BROTHER OF JOHN DEITZ IS WORKING FOR CLARENCE'S RELEASE.

## IS A BAILABLE CRIME

### Mob Violence Feared When Family Comes Into Court.—Cases Postponed to Oct. 19.

Hayward.—At least one member of the Deitz family will be at liberty and in a position to lend aid to his parents and brothers and sister, if the plans and intentions of William Deitz, a brother of John F. Deitz, materialize. Bail in any amount to $3,000 will be placed for Clarence Deitz who will appear before J. F. Riordan of municipal court on two warrants, one charging him with assault with intent to

# DIETZS MUST FACE MURDER CHARGE

## CAMERON DAM DEFENDERS KILLED DEPUTY HARP, SAYS CORONER.

## CLARENCE DARROW TO DEFEND

### Aid of Famous Socialist Lawyer of Chicago Sought—Great Legal Battle Expected for County.

Hayward, Wis., Oct. 11.—Charges of murder were preferred against John Deitz and wife and their son, Leslie, in the verdict of the coroner's jury at the inquest over Oscar Harp, the Winter deputy.

# Chapter XVI

The trial opened May 1st, 1911 at Hayward. My father was charged with the murder of Oscar Harp, the crime alleged to have been committed on October 9, 1910, when the Dietz home was raided. We had only the lawyers from the Milwaukee Defense Committee to defend him. Soon after the trial began the defense swore prejudice against the judge who was hearing the case and Judge Reed, of Wausau, presided thereafter.

My father felt confident that he would be proved innocent and would be back at our Rice Lake home in a few days, a free man. He knew he had not killed Harp—he knew that his only crime lay in protecting the rights of himself and his family—he had injured no man, beyond a trifling "fistic encounter," he felt, as he had said in Minneapolis, that right was stronger than might!

But it wasn't.

In just seven days the jury found him guilty and the judge sentenced him to life imprisonment in Waupun. He was taken to the penitentiary that same night to begin his sentence.

All in vain was the great tide of public sentiment! All in vain was the testimony of Captain Kane, the famous gun expert, which came as such a surprise to the state, who had employed him.

A bullet, alleged to have been the bullet which killed Harp, was taken to Captain Kane by the Sawyer County District Attorney, along with the thirty-thirty rifle owned by my father. Captain Kane spent several weeks in preparing his testimony. He made a trip to our farm, and had his companion to creep on his hands and knees toward the piles of lumber while he tried to sight him with the rifle from the barn, the point from which the state claimed my father killed Harp. The bullet was weighed and measured, after the expert's manner, and at last he proclaimed his findings completed, but kept them secret until the trial.

Doctor Grafton, county coroner, the same doctor who had visited me when I lay shot at Winter, and left morphine pills for me without examining my wounds, testified to finding the bullet in the dead man. He said the bullet had entered his mouth, passed down the throat and lodged under the shoulder blade, from where it was probed by the coroner after his death. Dr. Grafton testified that the bullet which had been given Captain Kane was the identical bullet which had been taken from the body.

Captain Kane was crippled and had to be accompanied by his personal physician everywhere he went. But he was called in on all questions pertaining to bullets in murder trials all over the country for his keen unbiased testimony was considered absolutely reliable. He has since died, and the world has lost a great firearms expert.

I can see him now as he took the stand to testify—a short, dark man walking on crutches. No one in the courtroom had any idea what his testimony would be! To the great surprise of everyone his findings were all in my father's favor.

He testified that the bullet could not have been shot from my father's gun—the bullet was too heavy for thirty-thirty ammunition. Second: The creasings on the bullet given him by the District Attorney did not correspond, to the creasings of my father's gun bore, nor to the creasings on other bullets which he fired from my father's gun in tests made at the farm.

Third: In his trip to the farm, he had not found a single point of the barn from which my father could have seen a man crawling toward the lumber piles, unless my father had stood upright in a trap door at the peak of the barn roof, as the topography of the land hid the lumber piles from the barn. Had my father climbed to the roof of the barn—which was most unlikely for the roof was peppered with bullets—he would have presented himself to the unrestricted view of the men shooting from ambush on every side. It might have been brought out that he did just that and that was why he was wounded in the hand, but previous testimony had brought out the fact that the man who shot him in the hand saw him at the little rear window of the barn when he fired. Furthermore, the haymow was only half filled with hay and to climb to the roof peak inside my father would have needed a ladder and we hadn't a single ladder on the farm.

Fourth: Assuming that my father had been able to shoot from the barn from some unknown place, the bullet could not have passed through the victim's body in the course indicated by the coroner. If Harp had been crawling with his head down, when the bullet entered his mouth, it would have passed out at the back of his neck and not lodged under his shoulder blade.

Fifth: The bullet given Captain Kane by the District Attorney was a ricocheted bullet and could have been fired from any direction.

Captain Kane testified that if it had ever entered the body of a man it had done so after it had struck a rock and had glanced sharply to one side or the other.

Father Pilon had told the press that the men were in ambush all around our clearing and had been cross firing from every direction throughout the day. The firing was so rapid and unsupervised that it was great wonder many of the posse were not injured by their companions according to the statements of Father Pilon and others who were present during the siege. They also repeated many times that not a shot was fired from the house, to their knowledge.

Captain Kane's testimony came as a distinct shock to the state, and immediately after he left the stand he was ousted by the attorneys for the state and told to go back to Milwaukee on the next train.

The strangest part of the whole affair was the complete absence of any murdered man's body on the farm at the time the shooting was alleged to have taken place. The reporters didn't see it, there were no photographs taken with an "X" marking the spot where the dead man lay, as reporters so love to publish. The records of Sawyer County contained no burial certificate and no record of a coroner's inquest over a dead body, although the coroner stated on the witness stand that one had been held the night the Dietz family was taken to jail. He further testified that the body of Oscar Harp was taken to his old home at Spring Green, Wisconsin.

Months later we lectured at Spring Green, and from a public platform we told our story and begged anyone who could give us any information of Oscar Harp, or tell us where in the vicinity of the village he was buried, to please meet us at our hotel. Not a person responded to our request.

Oscar Harp's alleged widow occupied a prominent place during the trial, sitting dry eyed in her widow's weeds while they recited the circumstances of her husband's supposed death.

Immediately after the trial she went west, and reports reached us later from several sources that acquaintances had found her and Mr. Harp happily reunited and living in comfort on a neat sum of money they had received for the death hoax. We tried to find them, but whoever it was, they moved quickly from place to place, and we never caught up with them.

We children had often discussed the Harps that summer and autumn of 1910. The pair had come there in the spring and settled in a little tar paper house on a little piece of land on the outskirts of Winter, which we passed every time we went into town for the mail. They were well dressed and looked so superior to their environment that considerable comment was aroused. They planted only a little patch of garden truck, and Mr. Harp never looked for work, and in a little community, naturally that excited some talk. As the autumn came on, we noticed they made no repairs to the thin little shack, and we young folks worried and fretted over the way the poor Harps would suffer when winter came every time we went to town.

Mrs. Harp came into the hotel the night I was shot and sat beside my bed for several hours, although I had never even spoken to the woman. She never even gave me a word of sympathy, just sat looking at me with hard black eyes! Quite a contrast to Mrs. Phelan's busy friendliness.

It is our contention that the Harps were brought into the village of Winter for the express purpose of staging a "death act" when the Dietz farm would be raided. We maintain that Mr. Harp was not killed, and that no man met death from my father's rifle that day or any other day.

It was rumored—and we prefer to believe this rumor—that a body was shipped into Winter from Chicago the day after Harp was supposed to have been shot, and that body was taken elsewhere by Mrs. Harp as her husband's remains.

But despite the over-whelming evidence in my father's favor he was sent to prison for life!

Then the fight began to get him pardoned or released!

Our first move was to take the case to the Supreme Court at Madison.

We had been advised to get Maurice McKenna, of Fond du Lac, as his ability was well known. Accordingly, the day after the trial my mother, Clarence, Leslie and I went to Fond du Lac. When we reached there we were told that we should make our home with the Peterson family during our stay. The Peterson family consisted of Mr. and Mrs. Sam Peterson, two daughters, Alma and Emma, and a son, Roloff. and how good they were to us! The day we arrived we made arrangements with Mr. McKenna, and started negotiations to hire James Malone of Juneau, and E. H. Nabor, of Mayville as his assistant. Briefs had to be prepared from the records of the trial, and an infinite amount of copying and tracing done. But inside of twenty-four hours this work was under way.

The day after our arrival Clarence suffered an attack of appendicitis and for days he was not expected to live. My mother spent most of her time at the hospital and I helped about the house. It seemed quite an imposition on the Peterson family, but they were kindness itself to us and wouldn't take a cent of room or board from us. We remained there three weeks and when Clarence was able to leave the hospital he was also taken there for his convalescence.

The problem of a permanent home for us was thoroughly discussed. We wanted to be near my father and near the lawyers who were working for his freedom, and the town of Mayville was finally chosen to be our home. We went there as the guests of the C. W. Doctor home, for Mr. Doctor was a friend of my father, and spent two weeks looking for a house. We finally decided upon a neat little six-room house, which we furnished with contributions from the Doctor and Nabor homes, and a few pieces of cheap furniture which we were able to buy. We were able to get a few items of household furnishing from our old home at Cameron Dam, and a small quantity of miscellaneous china. Most of our stuff had been stolen as souvenirs after the family was taken away, so there was very little that we could use in the new home at Mayville. However, it was a home! And we were again together after Clarence recovered enough to make the trip to Mayville. He spent the summer trying to get well again, but Leslie and I made a few trips out into the state to appear at theatres with our pictures and our little talks. We could have made plenty of money with our appearances, but there was much business with the lawyers to be talked over and when any new subject came up my mother thought we should be on hand to enter the discussion. Consequently she was constantly sending for us, and our time was so broken up that we did well to make the living expenses for the family. The lumber we had left on the Cameron Dam farm ready for the new home was sold, with the exception of a small quantity which was shipped to Mayville for the construction of a garage. The money obtained by its sale was turned over to the lawyers who were preparing my father's case for the Supreme Court. Thus my father realized not one iota of pleasure or profit from the logs for which he had fought—for the Supreme Court sustained the findings of the lower court, when his case came up late that summer.

Clarence, Leslie and I worked in theatres in Minnesota all the winter of 1911, with frequent expeditions to the northern part of Michigan. There was such a demand for us that we had to split up and each of the boys played in different localities. I wasn't strong enough to travel alone, so I took turns with the boys, traveling first with Clarence in the towns where he was speaking, and then with Leslie. I was the chief attraction, and the boys would scrap over which could have me! We had a set at pictures accumulated from various photographers which Mr. Doctor made into stereoptican slides, and these were thrown on the screen while one of us stood and explained them with a pointer. Then I would give my little talk about being shot. It seemed that my shooting was the thing the public cared most about! The theatre managers asked us to stress that point, and we were willing to oblige.

Posters bearing our pictures would always be placed outside the theatre, together with a great banner announcing that Myra and Leslie or Clarence Dietz were there in person! And what crowds would pack the theatres! We were paid from forty to sixty per cent of the theatre's door receipts, and we were booked for every night, staying many times two full weeks at a theatre. We made plenty of money, but we just kept out enough for our bare expenses and sufficient clothing to make a good appearance. The rest was sent to my mother, so she could finance all the lawyers' demands and other expenses.

Francis McGovern was elected Governor of Wisconsin to succeed Governor Davidson. We felt that we might have a chance of getting a pardon for my father from Governor McGovern, and set about getting petitions signed.

We stopped our work in the theatres when the weather became warm and started going to fairs, home-comings, band concerts, band conferences, celebrations—in fact, any place and anywhere that people were gathered together. There we would put up a little booth or occupy a portion of some other person's booth, such as a cigar booth, and get signers to petitions to be sent to the Governor asking for my father's pardon. We would have our big flags draped over the entrance of the booth, with big banners announcing "The Dietz Children". Inside we would have petitions all legally drawn up on the correct forms with room for several hundred signatures, and men and women would write their names on them. If anyone was sufficiently interested to circulate a petition in his own neighborhood he would be given a form—and hundreds were sent out through the country in that manner. At the close of that summer, we had seventy-five thousand names on petitions. We wrote to the governor asking for a hearing, which was granted for a date late in the autumn.

The whole family attended the hearing, with our three lawyers. It was held in the big executive office and the governor sat beside the big table and heard our plea. He studied the petitions thoroughly, as well as the many other exhibits which were placed in evidence. A few days later he sent his report, and we were overjoyed to find that our father's sentence was reduced from life to twenty years.

At least that was a start! Now we could work for his full pardon.

The winter of 1912 Leslie, Clarence and I spent in Milwaukee. We showed our pictures and gave our lectures at practically every theatre in Milwaukee, being booked solid for twenty-one weeks. I had received some additional honors during the autumn by being crowned Queen of the Dodge County Fair at Beaver Dam, Wisconsin, the largest county fair in the United States, it is claimed. I was given a diamond ring, which I still treasure. Clarence, Leslie and I were working at the Davidson Theatre the week of the fair and someone entered my name because I was from Mayville, one of the smaller towns in Dodge County. I won by a large majority, with twenty-three other girls in the contest. It certainly helped our work in Milwaukee for it gave me a reputation for something more than being the daughter of John Dietz. I had become quite a personage in my own right!

In the spring of 1913 we worked in the smaller towns along the lake, and then our spring season was closed. We had made a good many thousand dollars by that time—and it had all been made through our own efforts, just as any theatrical person earns a living. There were no donations now—every nickel was earned! We bought a new home for our mother and little John and Helen, who were going to school in Mayville, and furnished it completely. We paid $5500 cash for the house and an extra lot-- the house was a brand new home, cream brick construction with green trimmings, and had twelve rooms with two baths.

In June, 1913, we made arrangements with the Advance Motion Picture Company, a branch of the old Essanay Company, to make a motion picture of our lives, using our farm at Cameron Dam as the location.

In July, my mother, the boys, the children and I with a group of twenty actors and a cameraman returned to Cameron Dam and made a moving picture of the feud and the final battle. It was the first time I had seen the farm since that day three years before when I had dressed in my new brilliantine mail order suit and started to town for the mail with my brothers! What a lot had happened since that day!

Competent actors took the rolls of my father and mother, my brother John took the part of my sister, Helen, and my brothers Clarence and Leslie played their own parts and I played my own. A tall actor took Father Pilon's part and another played the judge in

# DIETZ BATTLE

OF

## Cameron Dam

IN MOVING PICTURES

---

## In Our Big Water-Proof Tent
## Sunday, April 4th, 1914
## Des Moines Opera House
## Admission: 10¢

Battle at the John Dietz Home, where more than a thousand
bullets struck their Cabin

Still photo from
*The Dietz Battle of
Cameron Dam.*

ietz and the much disputed Cameron Dam

the trial scene. We drove our team and a surrey over the road where I had been shot to the exact spot where the men with blackened faces shot us from ambush and then handcuffed us. It was a good picture, really, and as we looked at it in its completed form it surely carried us back to those unhappy days, so natural were our "father" and "mother". The actual making of the picture was a pleasant experience—not the gruesome time we had anticipated. However, there was one wretched result of our little play-acting.

With John taking the part of Helen and waving the flag as Helen had done on that memorable day three years before, we needed another little child to play the role of "Baby Johnny". As luck would have it, a new dentist and his wife had come to town, pleasant young people and the parents of a dear little light haired girl about the age our Johnny was at the time of the raid. We told them we needed a child and they gladly offered their little girl to us for the "battle scene". They brought her out to the farm the day the stage-raid took place, and she was put in the corner while the fake bullets whistled about the cabin, just as Johnny had been placed. Then when the surrender was made, my "mother" caught her in her arms and carried her outside into the crowd of ferocious looking men who roughly handled their prisoners. The child was so frightened she began screaming and crying and although her mother and father rushed in to quiet her, she could not be soothed. They carried her away still crying and later that night she became ill and had to be taken to a hospital. She developed a nervous trouble which affected her spine and has been a cripple ever since. The Dietz children must have had strong nerves indeed to withstand the real shooting without harm, when mere make-believe could ruin the life of another child.

The moving picture of our life meant just another way of reaching the public to my brothers—but to me it was of tremendous importance. The camera man who accompanied the actors to do the "shooting" of the picture became my husband the following year. My bridal pictures of that event were the first moving pictures of a real wedding ever made, and were given as wide circulation as the stories of my father's feud. At the end of ten years the marriage was dissolved. During the years I was married, however, I never ceased my efforts to obtain my father's release.

The moving picture of the Cameron Battle was finished by October of that year, and the autumn of 1913 found us with something far more interesting than our old slides as we went about the theatres. Moving pictures were not so common as they are now, and ours was a three-reel feature picture of great importance. We paid $5000 for its production, but we took in many times that amount with it.

Petitions were again circulated in the early part of Governor Philipp's administration, and again we sat in the executive office and begged for our father's freedom. But Governor Philipp refused to pardon him, saying Governor McGovern had done enough until a greater length of time had elapsed.

We still showed our pictures until the war. Then Leslie went to war, Clarence remaining at home because he was the main support of the family.

After Leslie's return we took our old picture and started out again. It was not that we were greedy for money—but we had to keep my father's case before the public. We had to have petitions with thousands of names if the governor would even give us a hearing --and while the people were with us in our desire to get our father out of prison the petition had to be placed before them before their signatures could be obtained. It costs money to get petitions signed—the travelling, the printed forms and the legal angles which must be nicely adjusted. All these things were bringing our bank account lower and lower. Leslie ran the pictures for another year and then we felt that we had enough signatures and enough new evidence to warrant a hearing before another governor. We settled down to wait for the next election.

In the autumn of 1919 we sold our home in Mayville and my mother and the children moved into Milwaukee where the opportunities for their education were greater. Clarence was selling cars for an automobile concern in Milwaukee and Leslie obtained a position with another automobile company. But each month we made our regular visit to our father at Waupun.

In 1921 we wrote to Governor Blaine, who had just been elected, requesting another hearing. He replied that if we would give him the proper evidence in the proper form he would give us a hearing, after which he would make his decision as soon as possible. For the third time we took our lists of petition signatures and our lawyers and sat in the executive office with the Governor across the big table while our story was presented.

A week later Governor Blaine called me by long distance phone at midnight telling me to take my mother the next morning and go to Waupun to bring my father home! There was no sleep that night in the Dietz home.

It was pouring rain the next morning, but that didn't keep us from Waupun. We were there by nine o'clock. The Governor had sent the necessary papers for me to give to the Warden, and everything was in readiness for my father's departure. He was well dressed in a good gray suit, black shoes, good hat and new overcoat, all furnished by the prison. The warden and my father shook hands and laughed and talked like two old friends parting at a summer resort. Then we slipped out the back way through the gardener's gate for the front gate was besieged with reporters waiting for my father's appearance. Governor Blaine warned us that it would be better to keep my father in a quiet place for a time as the strain might be too great. He had not been well during the last year and a half of his imprisonment, many times he was in the hospital when we visited the prison on visitors' day and we were not allowed to see him. It was difficult matters to dodge reporters that day—so eager were they to see my father, but we did our best to keep my father from exciting interviews.

It was a happy family reunion we had that
night in Milwaukee—many friends came in to see
my father and it was a happy day indeed. We
appreciated Governor Blaine's kindness in
choosing that day to pardon him—it was just
ten years to the day from the time my father
entered the prison—and somehow, being pardoned
on that day took away the sting of that
terrible day when he was sentenced.

But the long imprisonment had seriously
affected my father's health. He had been a
model prisoner, with many privileges but he
felt that his whole trouble had been brought
about through no wrong
doing of his own, and it
made the years at
confinement even more
tedious. He lived just
three years after his
release from prison.
During that time he
visited Rice Lake
frequently, but never
again did he go to
Cameron Dam, although he
talked about it to
anyone who wished to
mention it. He was
buried at Rice Lake, in
the family burial
ground.

This ends the story of that staunch farmer,
who so firmly fought for his rights—and my
brothers and myself, whose lives were
endangered by his adherence to his principles
and whose early days were lived in a manner
vastly different from the usual youngsters due
to my father's stern, unyielding disposition,

have never for one moment criticized one action or one decision made by my father. He lived a righteous life, according to his ideals. He was strong and fearless—and we like to believe that his strength and fearlessness came from the clear conscience in which he delighted. He made but one mistake—and that was in his claim that right is always stronger than might. He found in the last thirteen years of his life that might is the stronger.

Inquiries come to the family almost daily asking what has become of the rest of the family and I will close my book with a few words about each of us.

My mother retained her own home in Milwaukee until a few months ago when she went to live with Helen. She is 65, but despite the strain of those bitter years she is quite well. She has done marvelously well in keeping the family united, and in bringing up little John and Helen.

Helen was married last August to George H. Knox, and she assists him in conducting the Knox Motor Sales company at 2653 Fond du Lac Avenue, Milwaukee. They have a large apartment above the sales room, where they live very happily and comfortably and my mother makes her home there with them.

It is difficult to think of "Baby Johnny" being a man—but he is, with a wife and Baby Johnny of his own. However, young John Dietz, Fourth, is called Jackie-Boy, and is idolized by the family because he is so much like his daddy. John conducts the John Dietz Motor Company at Wauwatosa, near Milwaukee. Their home is at Wauwatosa.

Leslie is president of the Dietz-Whitney Motor Sales, distributors of De Soto cars. He gave me a most delightful blond sister-in-law when he married Nellie Biggam, of Milwaukee, and they have a little blond girl, Dorothy Anne, now two and one half years old. Their home is at 712 Fifty-fifth Street.

Clarence conducts the Clarence Dietz Motor Sales, handling Nash cars, on North Avenue, Wauwatosa. He married Miss Anne Sweiger of Milwaukee seven years ago. As Mrs. Clarence Dietz she is keeping the Dietz name before the public, for she is widely known politically and socially. She was an alternate appointed to the national convention at Kansas City last year, and lectures on political subjects throughout the United States. They live at 425 Washington Circle, South Wauwatosa.

All of my brothers and my brother-in-law are prosperous, respected business men—but my brothers feel the call of their boyhood days every autumn and each year they go back to the old farm at Cameron Dam during the hunting season. They drive in over the road they helped build so many years ago, and although the old foot bridge is gone, the beavers have built a dam across the river almost at the very spot where the old bridge hung and there they walk across to the site of the old cabin. The house burned the year after we made our moving picture, but the farm still remains in my mother's possession.

As for myself, I've found life a most exciting adventure. I've had trouble with my health, for I've had to undergo three major operations as a result of the shooting in 1910. I've lost a few bits of my vertebra and considerable blood and a husband, but I've never lost my sense of humor. I seem to have inherited a good memory from my father, and I remember with infinite gratitude the kindness of thousands of friends whom I have met in my life. It is largely for the sake of those friends, who throughout the years have said, "Tell us something of your life at Cameron Dam", that this story was written. I have told the truth—and if the truth differs from the newspaper stories which old-timers recall it is the fault of the writers of that period—not me!

I may not be so prosperous as my brothers, but happiness cannot be counted in terms of finance. I expect to be married again next spring to a prominent Milwaukee bachelor, and when I'm dead and gone I hope the next chronicler of the Dietz fortunes and misfortunes can pick up my story where I am leaving off and say: "She lived happily ever after".

The End

Author's note: Myra *did* live happily ever after.

The stage experience Myra attained while raising funds and getting petitions signed for her father's release from prison resulted in a career. And, besides the starring role she played in the 3-reel, 35 mm film, *The Dietz Battle of Cameron Dam,* she played many supporting roles in a variety of films produced by her first husband, Eugene Newman.

One film in particular gained nationwide exposure. Her 1914 marriage to Newman was the first-ever wedding ceremony captured by a movie camera. This event, combined with her celebrity, caused the film to be widely shown in theater newsreels, popular in the day.

Later, she marketed her on-stage speaking skills to a variety of companies that needed kitchen appliances and similar products promoted at trade shows, county fairs, and at in-store demonstrations. Store managers capitalized on her fame and she began a career that had her traversing the nation for decades as a "home economist" before settling down with her fourth husband in Shamrock, Texas.

In 1970, the community of Winter, Wisconsin, held a midsummer celebration called the Dietz Pioneer Days. It featured dances, feasts,

games and a special July 4th parade featuring Myra and her younger brother John as parade marshals. Celebrated as heroes, she and John spoke on stage about the events regarding the siege of the family's Thornapple River farm. Before leaving town, Myra and her brother made a final trip to Cameron Dam, finding their former home in ruins. It was the first time Myra had been there since the film was shot in 1913 and last time she ever visited the place where she'd come of age.

Seven years later, Myra passed away at her home in Texas. She now rests in an unmarked grave near her dear sister, Helen Dietz Knox.

Mary Almira Dietz
1888 - 1977

## Bert Horel, Fred Thorbahn, and the $1,000 reward

On Election Day, 1910, an argument on the streets of Winter resulted in a fight between John Dietz and Bert Horel, a Chippewa Lumber and Boom Company foreman. Horel's friends interceded. The fight resulted in Dietz shooting Horel. The wound was not fatal.

Although the shooting was clearly done in self-defense, Dietz was accused of attempted murder. This was all the county board needed to approve a $1,000 dead-or-alive reward for Dietz. However, there was no public announcement of the reward. Thus, only *insiders* knew of it. Sheriff Madden chose to tell a friend, Fred Thorbahn. Thorbahn and another crony of Madden's, Roy Van Alstine, plotted to ambush Dietz on the day he usually went to the Winter Post Office each week.

But, on this particular Saturday, John Dietz stayed home. Instead of ambushing the father, Thorbahn shot both Myra and Clarence. One week later, he oversaw the siege on the Dietz farm for Madden. After John Dietz was captured, Thorbahn claimed he deserved the reward. Rumor held that he shared the money with Van Alstine and Madden. Another rumor surfaced that Thorbahn had received $20,000 from the lumber syndicate as well. His reputation worsened. Mysteriously, his small, general store in nearby Radisson burned down. Hoping to find a home where he could live beyond public scrutiny, he left for Montana and opened a mercantile store. But when people learned he was the man who'd shot Myra, they shunned his business. Thorbahn turned to drink. He soon died, perhaps suffering more than John Dietz, the man that he'd helped put in prison.

## More on Raynor's Stopping Place

Headquarters for early trappers, loggers and rivermen, the Raynor Stopping Place has an interesting history. The following passge is excerpted from an interview of Al Raynor that appeared in the *Chippewa Falls Gazette*, August 5, 1922:

"I came to Southern Sawyer County," said Mr. Raynor, "in the spring of 1867 from the east, with many other old soldiers of the Civil War who were leaving the east to take up homesteads or to do logging in Wisconsin. The place was then owned by Judge Hayward [Anthony Judson Hayward, (Jud), never a judge.] and McCord who had a logging camp across the river directly opposite the house here.

"Old Fred Weyerhaeuser stopped with me in the early days, many times, also William Carson. Edward Rutledge of Chippewa Falls was nearly always with Weyerhaeuser. We often fed 150 men and kept them over night in this place. You had to step high at night after stoppers retired as 100 often slept on the floor.

"Bill Price of Black River Falls came in and built a dam on the Brunet in the early seventies. This is still known as Price's dam. Hundreds of Indians used to travel up and down the river, going back and forth every day, thirty, forty, and fifty canoes at a time. The [women] always did the paddling."

Raynor's, once a haven for travelers, lumberjacks, trappers, and hunters, is now listed on the U.S. Register of Historic Places, It is privately owned and may be the oldest building still standing in Sawyer County, Wisconsin.

## PAUL COATES

LA Times, July 1, 1962

# Life Among the Lost and Found

He's another of the many who live by their wits in the shadow of Hollywood Blvd.

His associates know him as The Scavenger.

But he prefers The Searcher. It has a more dignified ring.

When you get to know the man, you learn that it's not just false vanity which prompts his preference. He's a lot more complex than a simple scavenger.

Along with the dozens of others who exist on the contents of trash barrels, he accepts with thanks the routine rewards of his probing — discarded, half-filled lunch bags, bottles with a 2-cent deposit on their necks, a piece of clothing or pair of worn shoes now and then.

★

Once, he found a felt hat with the name Eugene Biscailuz stenciled inside. It fit fine. Another time, he scavenged a ticket to a New York revue playing to sold-out crowds at Pantages Hollywood, and sat next to Alexander Pantages himself. There was the pair of the great Valentino's trousers salvaged from a cardboard box in an alley. They were too big, but they brought $5.

These are the common rewards of his trade. Or, hobby, as he prefers to call it. But it's the uncommon rewards he likes to talk about.

He likes to tell of the insight into the human animal he gains from his daily pursuit of other people's trash.

He found a thousand-dollar check from a bank in Canada once, tracked down its owner — a girl who worked in a beauty parlor—and walked away without being offered so much as a penny reward.

He has rescued diaries of girls trying to break into Hollywood, and stacks of old impassioned love letters. And he's read every one of them.

He found five gold medallions belonging to a famous model. He returned them. She said thanks. He found a scrapbook belonging to an actor

Cootes

who was on the way down. He saw the former star on the boulevard one afternoon and told him of his cache. The Searcher surrendered it and the actor slipped him a $10 bill.

★

But his most prized discovery came nearly 30 years ago. While sifting through a pile of boxes left for the junkman outside the office of an agent who had dropped dead of a heart attack, he came across a 146-page original manuscript.

It told the story of one of America's greatest symbols of rugged individualism—a raw-boned Wisconsin farmer named John Dietz. In the early 20th Century Dietz made national headlines month after month, as he continued his running battle with a lumbering company which moved in on his land.

He built a fortress, armed his sons and daughters, and withstood assaults by hired gunmen, posses and finally the militia in defending what was his. But the conspiracy against him was too big.

★

Eventually, he was captured and sentenced to life imprisonment for the "murder" of one of the men who tried to shoot him off his land. Dietz served 10 years of his sentence. Then a new state administration in Wisconsin gave him a full pardon and he returned to his farm to live out the last few years of his life.

The lumber company went broke while Dietz was in prison.

The long manuscript which The Searcher found was a detailed account of the man's battle "to defend his own," written by his daughter, Myra Dietz, who held a shotgun along side of him. Myra herself was shot once by paid thugs hiding in ambush as she drove her wagon to town.

She also led the battle to free her father.

For years, The Searcher has kept the daughter's vivid personal story of her father's heroism. He made several attempts to contact Myra Dietz over the years to tell her of his find.

One time, he thought he had located her in Texas. Another time, he thinks he just missed her when she visited Pasadena.

But he never found her.

★

If she's alive today, she's 73 years old.

The Searcher's no youngster himself anymore.

And that bothers him.

He wants Myra Dietz to get back her manuscript, but now—he knows—time is working against him.

# Myra's Memoir

Myra typed only one copy of her memoir, then began the arduous task of trying to tempt publishers to turn it into a book. But by 1929, the struggle at the farm was no longer newsworthy to the publishers she approached. Then came the Great Depression and book publishing languished along with most other industries.

During the Great Depression, a fellow scrounging through trashcans near a Los Angeles publisher's office the found her story. Upon reading it, he recognized the importance of the rejected manuscript. He tried for years to return it to her without success. Somehow, it ended up in the John Dietz collection of memorabilia at the Sawyer County Historical Society.

My husband's research for his book about Myra, *Thornapple Girl,* led him to Myra's long-lost memoir. Now, after languishing for over 91 years, Myra's account of her life is finally in print.

Below are images of Myra's original pages. They show some of the many changes she made prior to her submitting the manuscript.

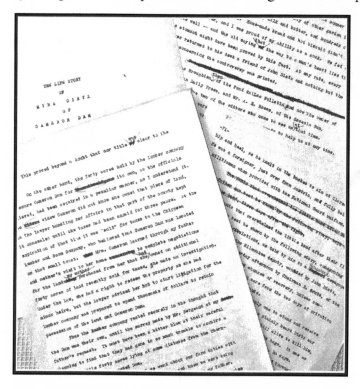